Summer Success®

Math

Andy Clark • Patsy F. Kanter

Great Source®
EDUCATION GROUP
A Division of Houghton Mifflin Company

CREDITS

Writing: Sherrill Bennington, Jeanne Goldman, Tabula Rasa Publishing

Design/Production: Taurins Design

Illustration: Debra Spina Dixon

Cover and Package Design: Kristen Davis/Great Source

Printed in the United States of America

International Standard Book Number–13: 978-0-669-53683-6

International Standard Book Number–10: 0–669–53683–0

8 9 10 1689 17 16 15 14
4500483775
Visit our web site: http://www.greatsource.com/

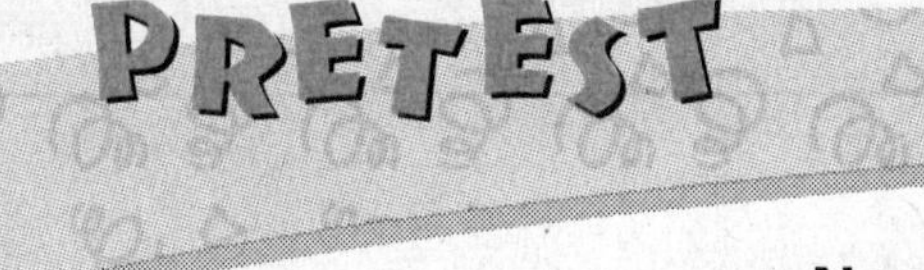

Name ______________________

NUMBER

Choose the best answer or write a response for each question.

1. Which diagram shows 0.1 of the stars shaded?

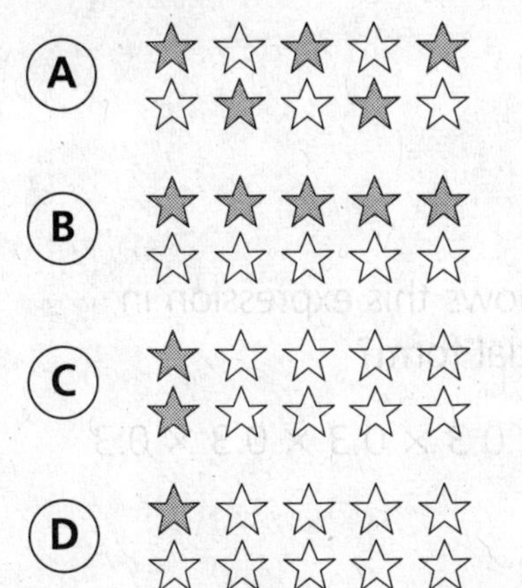

Ⓐ

Ⓑ

Ⓒ

Ⓓ

2. What is 0.25 written as a fraction?

Ⓐ $\frac{5}{2}$

Ⓑ $\frac{1}{2}$

Ⓒ $\frac{2}{5}$

Ⓓ $\frac{1}{4}$

3. What is $\frac{1}{3}$ written as a percent?

Ⓐ $33.\overline{3}\%$

Ⓑ $3.\overline{3}\%$

Ⓒ $\overline{3}.0\%$

Ⓓ $0.\overline{3}\%$

4. What is the opposite of the integer 5?

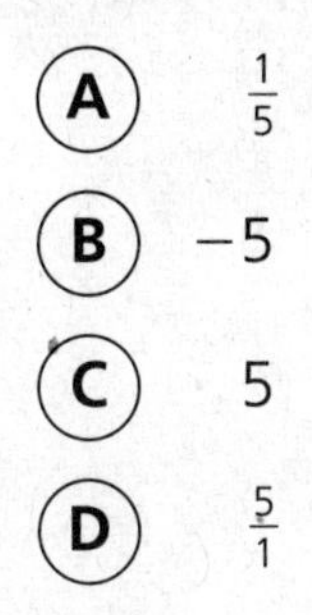

Ⓐ $\frac{1}{5}$

Ⓑ -5

Ⓒ 5

Ⓓ $\frac{5}{1}$

5. Which group of numbers is listed from least to greatest?

Ⓐ $-\frac{1}{8}, -\frac{1}{4}, \frac{1}{2}, \frac{1}{3}$

Ⓑ $\frac{1}{2}, \frac{1}{3}, -\frac{1}{4}, -\frac{1}{8},$

Ⓒ $-\frac{1}{4}, -\frac{1}{8}, \frac{1}{3}, \frac{1}{2}$

Ⓓ $-\frac{1}{4}, -\frac{1}{8}, \frac{1}{2}, \frac{1}{3}$

6. Which expression does **not** have the same value as the others?

Ⓐ -9×1

Ⓑ $|-9|$

Ⓒ $-3 \times (-3)$

Ⓓ 1×9

Name ______________________________

OPERATIONS

7. What is the difference?

$-56 - 31 =$ ____

(A) 87

(B) 25

(C) -25

(D) -87

8. What is $\sqrt{81}$?

(A) 9 and -9

(B) 9 only

(C) -9 only

(D) 81 and -81

9. What is the missing factor?

$-4 \times$ ____ $= 100$

(A) 25

(B) -25

(C) -50

(D) Not Given

10. What is the quotient?

$-\frac{1}{4} \div \frac{1}{4}$

(A) 4

(B) 1

(C) 0

(D) -1

11. Which shows this expression in exponential form?

$0.3 \times 0.3 \times 0.3 \times 0.3 \times 0.3$

(A) 0.3^{-5}

(B) 0.3^{5}

(C) 3.0^{5}

(D) 5.0^{3}

12. Which shows this number in scientific notation?

5,430,000

(A) 543×10^{4}

(B) 54.3×10^{5}

(C) 5.43×10^{6}

(D) 0.543×10^{7}

Name ____________________

PATTERNS AND ALGEBRA

13. Continue the pattern.

13, 9, 5, 1, −3, −7, ___

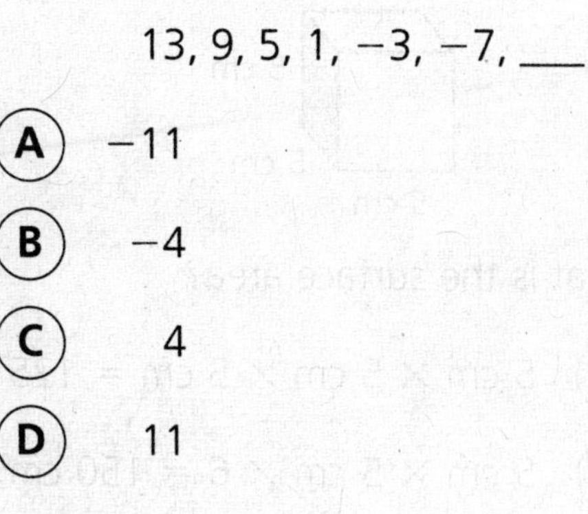

(A) −11

(B) −4

(C) 4

(D) 11

14. What rule is followed to create the pattern?

−20, −14, −8, −2, 4

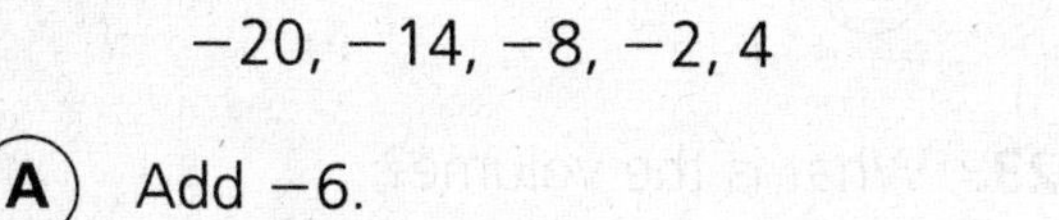

(A) Add −6.

(B) Add −4.

(C) Add 4.

(D) Add 6.

15. Write an equation to find the measure of the third angle.

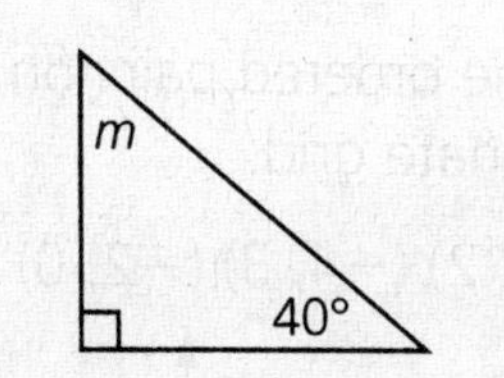

Answer: ____________________

16. Solve for n.

$\frac{1}{4}n = -12$

(A) $n = 48$

(B) $n = 3$

(C) $n = -3$

(D) $n = -48$

17. Use the grid to graph the equation.

$y = 2x + 1$

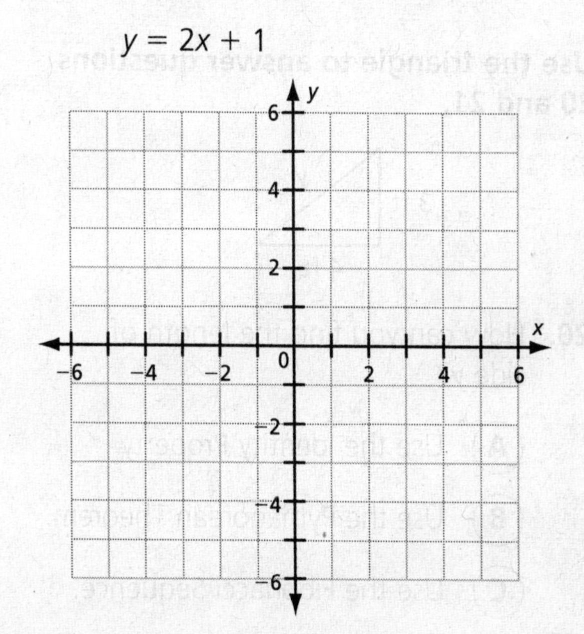

18. What is the slope of a line?

(A) the *y*-intercept

(B) the change in *x*-value

(C) the change in *y*-value

(D) the ordered pair (0, 0)

Name ______________________________

GEOMETRY AND MEASUREMENT

19. Which diagram shows a pair of supplementary angles?

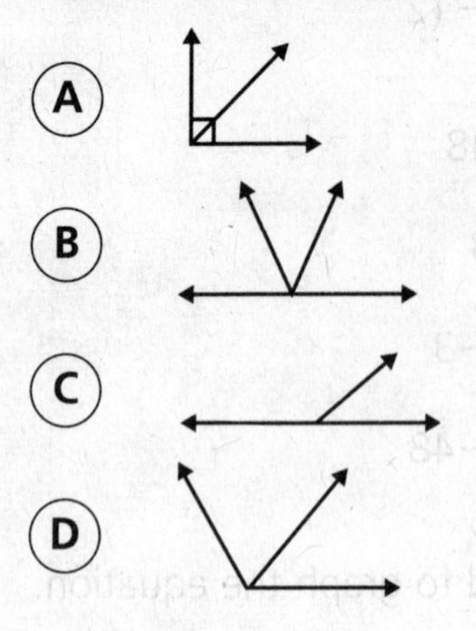

Use the triangle to answer questions 20 and 21.

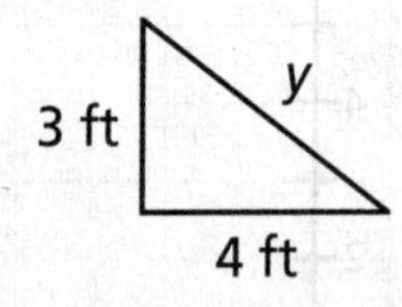

20. How can you find the length of side y?

(A) Use the Identity Property.

(B) Use the Pythagorean Theorem.

(C) Use the Fibonacci Sequence.

(D) Use the Golden Ratio.

21. What is the area of the triangle?

(A) $\frac{1}{2}(4 \text{ ft} \times 3 \text{ ft}) = 6 \text{ ft}^2$

(B) $4 \text{ ft} \times 3 \text{ ft} = 12 \text{ ft}^2$

(C) $\frac{1}{2}(4 \text{ ft} + 3 \text{ ft} + y) = \frac{7 \text{ ft} + y}{2}$

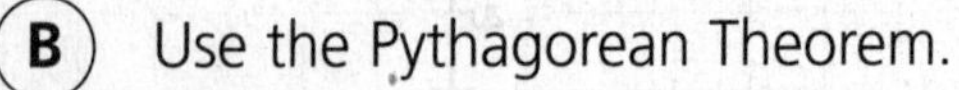

(D) $4 \text{ ft} + 3 \text{ ft} + y = 7 \text{ ft} + y$

Use the cube to answer questions 22 and 23.

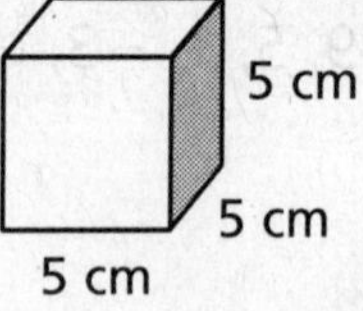

22. What is the surface area?

(A) $5 \text{ cm} \times 5 \text{ cm} \times 5 \text{ cm} = 125 \text{ cm}^3$

(B) $5 \text{ cm} \times 5 \text{ cm} \times 6 = 150 \text{ cm}^2$

(C) $5 \text{ cm} \times 5 \text{ cm} \times 3 = 75 \text{ cm}^2$

(D) $5 \text{ cm} + 5 \text{ cm} + 5 \text{ cm} = 15 \text{ cm}$

23. What is the volume?

(A) $5 \text{ cm} \times 5 \text{ cm} \times 5 \text{ cm} = 125 \text{ cm}^3$

(B) $5 \text{ cm} + 5 \text{ cm} + 5 \text{ cm} = 15 \text{ cm}$

(C) $5 \text{ cm} \times 5 \text{ cm} + 5 \text{ cm} = 25 \text{ cm}^2 + 5 \text{ cm}$

(D) $5 \text{ cm} + 5 \text{ cm} \times 5 \text{ cm} = 5 \text{ cm} + 25 \text{ cm}^2$

24. Plot the ordered pairs on the coordinate grid.

(3, 2) (−4, 3) (−2, 0) (4, −3)

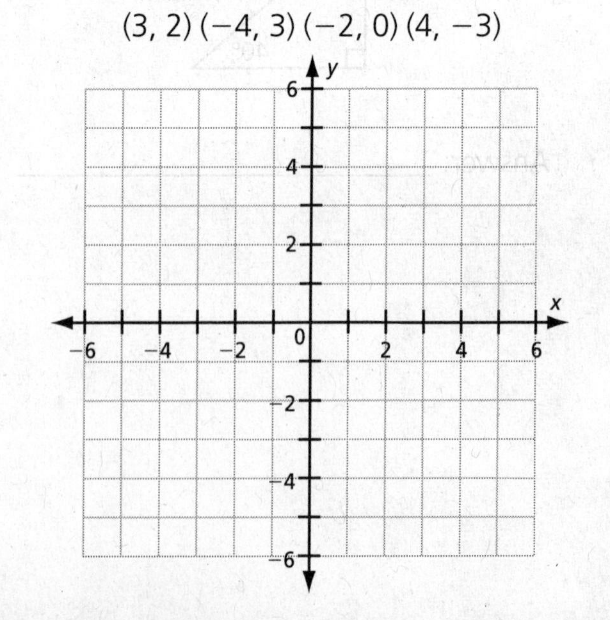

Name ______________________________

DATA

Use the stem-and-leaf plot to answer questions 25–28.

Running Times (sec)

Stems	Leaves
9	1 1 4
8	0 2 5 5
7	0 4 5 5

25. Make a key that shows that the stems are tens and the leaves are ones.

Answer: ______________________________

26. What is the median of the running times?

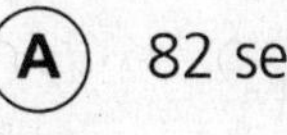
Ⓐ 82 seconds

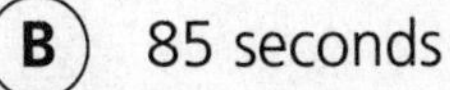
Ⓑ 85 seconds

Ⓒ 90 seconds

Ⓓ 95 seconds

27. What is the mean running time?

Ⓐ 94 seconds

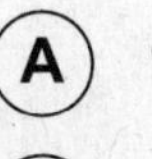
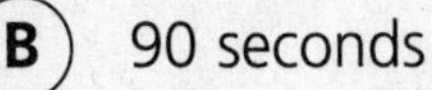
Ⓑ 90 seconds

Ⓒ 85 seconds

Ⓓ 82 seconds

28. Make a line plot with the running times.

29. If there are 6 red counters, 3 blue ones, and 2 green ones in a bag, what is the probability that you'll pick a red counter?

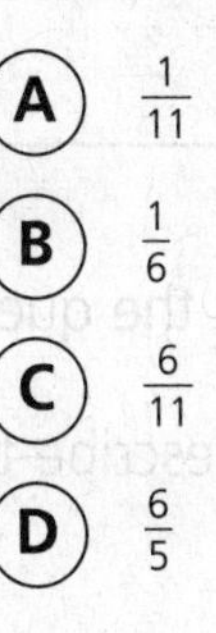
Ⓐ $\frac{1}{11}$

Ⓑ $\frac{1}{6}$

Ⓒ $\frac{6}{11}$

Ⓓ $\frac{6}{5}$

30. Which kind of graph is best for showing change over time?

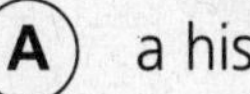
Ⓐ a histogram

Ⓑ a line graph

Ⓒ a circle graph

Ⓓ a box-and-whisker plot

Name ____________________

PROBLEM SOLVING

31. Each variable stands for one, and only one, integer. Find the values of a, b, and c.

$a + 2 = b$

$c - 2 = b$

$a + b = 12$

Show your work.

Answer: ____________________

32. Use the diagram to answer the questions.

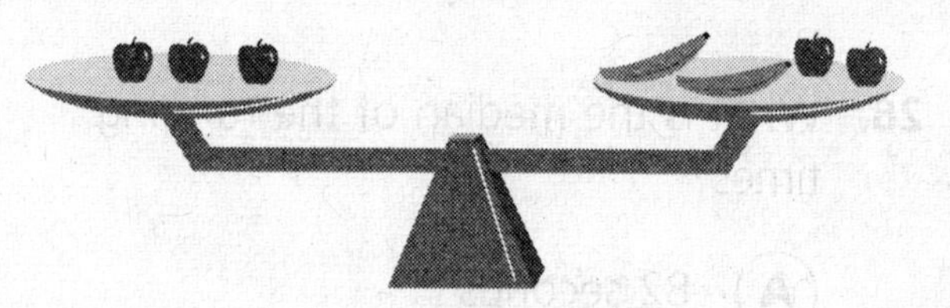

A. Write an equation to describe the diagram. Show your work.

Answer: ____________________

B. What is the weight of 1 banana in terms of apples? Show your work.

Answer: ____________________

C. What is the weight of 1 apple in terms of bananas? Show your work.

Answer: ____________________

PRACTICE TODAY'S NUMBER 0.1

Name ____________________

NUMBER AND OPERATIONS

Shade each model to show the decimal or percent. ◂1–2. MOC 012, 3–4. MOC 442

1. 0.1 of the grid

2. 0.1 of the circles

3. 10% of the circles

4. 10% of this circle

Write the word form for each number. ◂5–8. MOC 012, 022

5. 0.1 ____________________

6. 0.10 ____________________

7. 0.6 ____________________

8. 1.1 ____________________

PATTERNS AND ALGEBRA

Continue the pattern and answer the related questions. ◂9–11. MOC 204

9. 0.1, 0.2, 0.3, 0.4, 0.5, ______, ______, ______

10. If the pattern continues, what is the tenth term? ____________

11. Write an expression for finding the hundredth term. ____________

GEOMETRY AND MEASUREMENT

Use the diagram for exercises ◂12–14. MOC 348–354

12. What is the perimeter of this triangle? ____________

13. What are the measures of the angles in the triangle? ____________

0.1 cm

14. Draw a 3-sided closed figure with a right angle and 2 congruent sides. Name the figure. Be as specific as possible.

____

REVIEW

List all of the factors of these numbers. ◂15–18. MOC 056

15. 12 ____________________

16. 20 ____________________

17. 24 ____________________

18. 36 ____________________

Use >, <, or = to compare the fractions. ◂19–22. MOC 032, 036, 039–040, 048–049

19. $\frac{1}{4}$ ______ $\frac{3}{4}$

20. $\frac{1}{2}$ ______ $\frac{5}{10}$

21. $\frac{3}{8}$ ______ $\frac{5}{8}$

22. $\frac{2}{3}$ ______ $\frac{3}{4}$

GLOSSARY TO GO

Today, you will begin to create a math glossary to be used in school and at home. It will contain pictures and definitions of many math terms that you will encounter in math texts and tests. By writing your own definitions and keeping them in this book, you will be more likely to remember and understand these terms. You can use the glossary throughout the summer and as a resource during the next school year.

DIRECTIONS

- Put a marker or a self-stick note on page 151 of this book.
- Each day, write definitions and draw pictures illustrating new math terms. The vocabulary should be covered in your class time, so you should be familiar with most of the terms.

GAME

Decimal Targets

Object: Write and evaluate 3 addition expressions with sums close to, but less than, 10.

MATERIALS

2 sets of 0–9 Digit Cards, pencils

DIRECTIONS

1. Shuffle the Digit Cards and place them in a facedown stack. Decide who is Player 1. If you are Player 2, turn to page 10. Both of you will use this recording sheet.
2. If you are Player 1, draw 7 Digit Cards and write a digit in each space in the *Expression* column of your recording sheet. **Tell how you decided** how to place the digits. **(I don't want my score to go over 10, so I'll make sure that I don't have 10 tenths.)**
3. Write your sum. Then, find the difference between your sum and the target and write it in the *Running Total* column. If your score is closer to 10, you win the round.
4. If you are Player 2, draw your cards while Player 1 is working.
5. Shuffle all of the cards after each round and switch who draws first. After 3 rounds, if your running total is closer to 0, you win the game. After several games, you may change the target number.

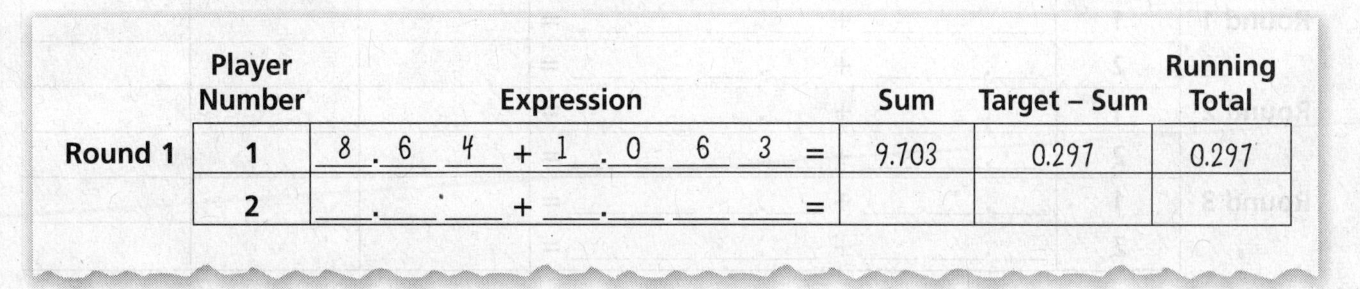

	Player Number	Expression	Sum	Target – Sum	Running Total
Round 1	1	8 . 6 4 + 1 . 0 6 3 =	9.703	0.297	0.297
	2	__ . __ __ + __ . __ __ __ =			

Decimal Targets Recording Sheet

	Player Number	Expression	Sum	Target – Sum	Running Total
Round 1	1	___.___ ___ ___ + ___.___ ___ ___ =			
	2	___.___ ___ ___ + ___.___ ___ ___ =			
Round 2	1	___.___ ___ ___ + ___.___ ___ ___ =			
	2	___.___ ___ ___ + ___.___ ___ ___ =			
Round 3	1	___.___ ___ ___ + ___.___ ___ ___ =			
	2	___.___ ___ ___ + ___.___ ___ ___ =			

	Player Number	Expression	Sum	Target – Sum	Running Total
Round 1	1	___.___ ___ ___ + ___.___ ___ ___ =			
	2	___.___ ___ ___ + ___.___ ___ ___ =			
Round 2	1	___.___ ___ ___ + ___.___ ___ ___ =			
	2	___.___ ___ ___ + ___.___ ___ ___ =			
Round 3	1	___.___ ___ ___ + ___.___ ___ ___ =			
	2	___.___ ___ ___ + ___.___ ___ ___ =			

	Player Number	Expression	Sum	Target – Sum	Running Total
Round 1	1	___.___ ___ ___ + ___.___ ___ ___ =			
	2	___.___ ___ ___ + ___.___ ___ ___ =			
Round 2	1	___.___ ___ ___ + ___.___ ___ ___ =			
	2	___.___ ___ ___ + ___.___ ___ ___ =			
Round 3	1	___.___ ___ ___ + ___.___ ___ ___ =			
	2	___.___ ___ ___ + ___.___ ___ ___ =			

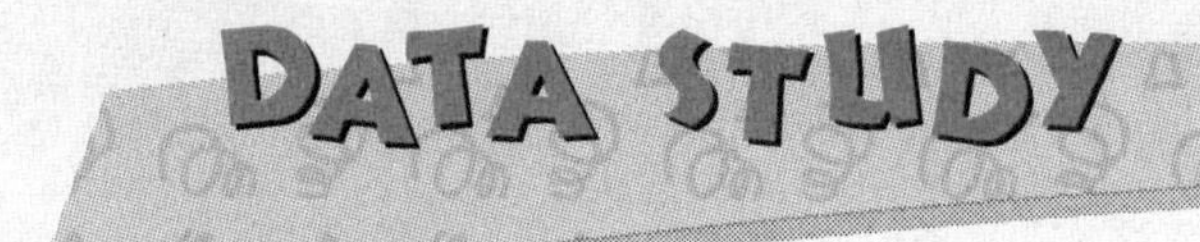

Name ______________________

Making a Line Plot

How fast are the world's fastest runners?

DIRECTIONS

- Work with a partner. One of you turn to page 12, where you will complete your plot.
- Complete the table.
- Decide how to label your number line to represent the data.
- Title your plot and plot the data.
- Answer the questions to analyze the data.

Men's 400-Meter Run
2004 Summer Olympics

Name	Time (seconds)	Rounded Time
Alleyne, Francique	44.66	
Blackwood, Michael	45.55	
Brew, Derrick	44.42	
Clarke, Davian	44.83	
Djhone, Leslie	44.94	
Harris, Otis	44.16	
Simpson, Brandon	44.76	
Wariner, Jeremy	44.00	

Source: Boston.com/Sports

ANALYZE THE DATA

1. Where is there a cluster of data on the line plot?

____

2. Write 2 facts about the data. You may want to consider the range, mean, and median.

____

____

3. Use the table to find the mean time to the nearest hundredth of a second. Compare the mean to the median time.

Mean: ____________

Median: ____________

The mean and median ______________________.

Making a Line Plot

Title: ______________________________

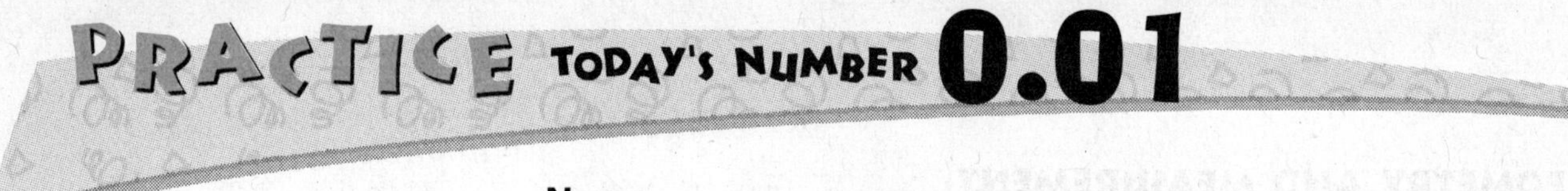

Name ______________________________

NUMBER AND OPERATIONS

Shade each model to show the decimal. ◄1–2. MOC 012

1. 0.01

2. 0.14

Answer each question. ◄3–4. MOC 443

3. What is 1% of $1.00? ______________

4. What is 1% of 125? ______________

Solve the problems. ◄5–7. MOC 445

5. If 1.1 is 1% of a number, what is the number? ______________

6. If one hundredth of a number is 10, what is the number? ______________

7. Don spent 99% of his money. He had $1.00 left. How much money did he start with?

____

PATTERNS AND ALGEBRA

Continue the pattern and answer the related questions. ◄8–10. MOC 204

8. 10,000; 100; 1; __________; __________

9. If this pattern continues, what is the seventh term? ______________

10. Describe the rule for this pattern.

____

____

____

GEOMETRY AND MEASUREMENT

Use the diagram for exercises 11–13. ◂11–13. MOC 331, 342, 353

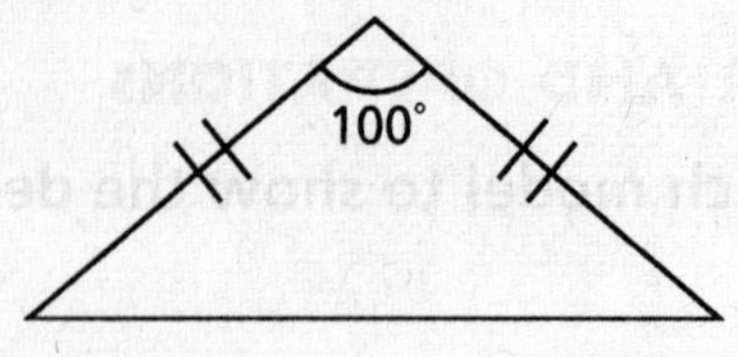

11. Name the figure. Be as specific as possible.

____

12. What can you tell about the size of the remaining angles just by looking at them?

____

13. What is the sum of the remaining 2 angles of this triangle? __________

REVIEW

Multiply by powers of 10. ◂14–17. MOC 144

14. $10 \times 6 =$ __________

15. $1{,}000 \times 66 =$ __________

16. $100 \times 60 =$ __________

17. $1{,}000 \times 101 =$ __________

Multiply by powers of 10 less than one. ◂18–21. MOC 151, 178

18. $\frac{1}{10}$ of 200 = __________

19. $\frac{1}{10}$ of 16 = __________

20. 0.1 of 50 = __________

21. $0.1 \times 24 =$ __________

GLOSSARY TO GO

Write definitions and draw pictures illustrating new math terms. The vocabulary should be covered in your class time, so you should be familiar with most of the terms.

Name ____________________

Making a Stem-and-Leaf Plot

How much faster is an Olympic champion than his competitors?

DIRECTIONS

- Work with a partner. One of you turn to page 16, where you will complete your plot.
- Decide how you will divide the numbers into stems and leaves, and what will be the stems for your stem-and-leaf plot.
- Title your plot and plot the data.
- Write a key that explains how to read the stems and leaves.
- Answer the questions to analyze the data.

Men's 400-Meter Run
2004 Summer Olympics

Name	Time (seconds)
Alleyne, Francique	44.66
Blackwood, Michael	45.55
Brew, Derrick	44.42
Clarke, Davian	44.83
Djhone, Leslie	44.94
Harris, Otis	44.16
Simpson, Brandon	44.76
Wariner, Jeremy	44.00

Source: Boston.com/Sports

ANALYZE THE DATA

1. Where did most of the times fall on the stem-and-leaf plot? ____________________
2. Use your plot to find the fastest, slowest, and median times. Then find the range and compare the fastest time to the median time.

   Fastest: ______________

   Slowest: ______________

   Median: ______________

   Range: ______________

   The fastest time was ______________ faster than the slowest time

   and ______________ faster than the median time.
3. Compare your stem-and-leaf plot with the line plot of the same data on page 12. What are the benefits of using each type of plot?

   ____

   ____

Making a Stem-and-Leaf Plot

Title: ______________________________

Stem	Leaves

Key: ______________________________

PRACTICE TODAY'S NUMBER 0.125

Name ______________________________

NUMBER AND OPERATIONS

Shade each model to show the decimal, fraction, or percent. ◀1–2. MOC 012, 442

1. 0.125 of the grid

2. $12\frac{1}{2}$% of the circles

Write each fraction or decimal as a percent. ◀3–6. MOC 026, 043, 442

3. $\frac{1}{8}$ __________

4. $\frac{3}{8}$ __________

5. 0.375 __________

6. 0.875 __________

Solve the problem. ◀7. MOC 443

7. A basketball player makes about 37.5% of her shots. If she shoots 32 times, about how many times will the ball go into the basket? Show your work.

____

PATTERNS AND ALGEBRA

Continue the pattern and answer the related questions. ◀8–10. MOC 204

8. 1.0, 1.125, 1.25, __________, __________, __________

9. If this pattern continues, what is the tenth term? __________

10. How can you find the twentieth term?

____

GEOMETRY AND MEASUREMENT

Use the diagram. ◀11. MOC 342 12. MOC 351, 353

11. Describe how you can find the measure of the third angle in a triangle when you know the measures of 2 of the angles.

____

____

12. Name the figure and label all of the angles.

____

REVIEW

Find each product. ◀13–24. MOC 144, 158–161

13. $\frac{1}{100}$ of 100 = ________

14. $\frac{1}{100}$ of 300 = ________

15. $\frac{1}{100}$ of 3,000 = ________

16. $\frac{3}{100}$ of 100 = ________

17. $\frac{3}{100}$ of 300 = ________

18. $\frac{3}{100}$ of 3,000 = ________

19. $0.01 \times 100 =$ ________

20. $0.01 \times 500 =$ ________

21. $0.01 \times 5{,}000 =$ ________

22. $0.03 \times 100 =$ ________

23. $0.03 \times 500 =$ ________

24. $0.03 \times 5{,}000 =$ ________

GLOSSARY TO GO

Write definitions and draw pictures illustrating new math terms. The vocabulary should be covered in your class time, so you should be familiar with most of the terms.

Winning Percent

Object: Cover 4 percents in a row by making their equivalent fractions.

MATERIALS

Winning Percent Game Board, 2 sets of 0–9 Digit Cards (discard the 0 and 7 cards), counters: 10 each of 2 colors

$22\frac{2}{9}\%$	$83\frac{1}{3}\%$	20%	$66\frac{2}{3}\%$	$33\frac{1}{3}\%$	100%
50%	$33\frac{1}{3}\%$	50%	12.5%	75%	$44\frac{4}{9}\%$
25%	$11\frac{1}{9}\%$	25%	50%	$33\frac{1}{3}\%$	60%
50%	75%	62.5%	100%	$66\frac{2}{3}\%$	37.5%
100%	80%	$66\frac{2}{3}\%$	$55\frac{5}{9}\%$	62.5%	25%
75%	$16\frac{2}{3}\%$	20%	50%	40%	$88\frac{8}{9}\%$

DIRECTIONS

1. Choose the counter color to mark your plays. Decide who is Player 1.
2. Shuffle the Digit Cards and place them facedown by the Game Board.
3. Draw 3 cards and form a fraction with any 2 digits. The value of your fraction must be less than or equal to 1. Place one of your counters on the Game Board on the percent equivalent to your fraction. **Tell how you decided** where to put your counter. **(I want to block you, so I can't use $\frac{1}{9}$ or $\frac{5}{9}$. I can use $\frac{1}{5}$ to cover 20%.)** Place the Digit Cards in a discard pile.
4. Take turns. When there are no more cards in the facedown pile, shuffle the cards in the discard pile and continue to play. If there is nowhere to place your counter, you lose your turn.
5. The first player to get 4 counters in a row vertically, horizontally, or diagonally wins.

This one is easy. I know that $\frac{1}{5} = \frac{2}{10}$ and $\frac{2}{10} = \frac{20}{100}$. My counter goes on 20%.

Name ______________________________

Problem Solving with Ratios: Perimeter

DIRECTIONS

- Rewrite each problem in your own words.
- Solve the problem. Circle the strategies you use.
- Show your work and complete the answer. Don't forget the units.

POSSIBLE STRATEGIES

- Guess, Check, and Revise
- Write an Equation
- Make a Model or a Diagram
- Other: ____________

PROBLEM 1

The perimeter of a rectangle is 110 centimeters. The length is 10 times the width, so the ratio of the length to the width is 1 to 0.1. What are the dimensions of the rectangle?

The dimensions of the rectangle are ____________________.

PROBLEM 2

A rectangle has a perimeter of 101 centimeters. The ratio of the length to the width is 1 to 0.01. What are the dimensions of the rectangle?

The dimensions of the rectangle are ____________________.

ANALYZE YOUR WORK

1. Did your work on the first problem help you with the second problem? If so, how?

____

2. If you did not use the *Write an Equation* strategy, try to write one now for Problem 2.

____

PRACTICE TODAY'S NUMBER $0.\overline{3}$

Name ____________________

NUMBER AND OPERATIONS

Write each percent or fraction. ◄1–4. MOC 024, 442

1. Write $\frac{1}{3}$ as a percent ____________

2. Write $\frac{2}{3}$ as a percent. ____________

3. Write 0.16 as a fraction. ____________

4. Write $0.8\overline{3}$ as a fraction. ____________

Write an equation to solve the problem. ◄5–6. MOC 241

5. The school soccer team won $\frac{2}{3}$ of the games they played. They lost 8 games. How many games did they play altogether?

____

6. A CD is on sale for $\frac{1}{3}$ off the original price. It costs $12 on sale. What was the original price of the CD?

____

PATTERNS AND ALGEBRA

Use the pattern to solve. ◄7–9. MOC 204

7.

8. If the pattern above continues, draw a picture of the tenth figure.

9. Describe the pattern for the *n*th figure.

____

____

MEASUREMENT

Write the number of inches in each measure. ◂10–13. MOC 160–161, 536

10. How many inches are in $\frac{1}{3}$ of a foot? __________

11. How many inches are in $\frac{2}{3}$ of a foot? __________

12. How many inches are in $\frac{1}{3}$ of a yard? __________

13. How many inches are in $\frac{2}{3}$ of a yard? __________

REVIEW

Find each product or quotient. ◂14–24. MOC 144, 158–159, 175, 184–186

14. $25 \times 10 =$ __________

15. $25 \times 1 =$ __________

16. $25 \times 0.1 =$ __________

17. $25 \times 0.01 =$ __________

18. $25 \times 0.001 =$ __________

19. $25 \div 10 =$ __________

20. $25 \div 1 =$ __________

21. $25 \div 0.1 =$ __________

22. $25 \div 0.01 =$ __________

23. $25 \div 0.001 =$ __________

24. What question is $25 \div 0.01$ asking?

____

GLOSSARY TO GO

Write definitions and draw pictures illustrating new math terms. The vocabulary should be covered in your class time, so you should be familiar with most of the terms.

Name ______________________________

Problem Solving with Ratios: Mystery Numbers

DIRECTIONS

- Discuss each problem with your partner.
- Solve the problem. Circle the strategies you use.
- Show your work and complete the answer.

POSSIBLE STRATEGIES

- Guess, Check, and Revise
- Write an Equation
- Make a Model or a Diagram
- Other: ____________

PROBLEM 1

There are 2 numbers. One number is 0.25 of the other number. Their sum is 30. What are the numbers?

The numbers are __________ and __________.

PROBLEM 2

There are 2 numbers. One number is 0.125 of the other number. Their sum is 45. What are the numbers?

The numbers are __________ and __________.

ANALYZE YOUR WORK

1. Did your work on the first problem help you with the second problem? If so, how?

____

2. If you did not use the *Write an Equation* strategy, try to write one now for Problem 2.

____

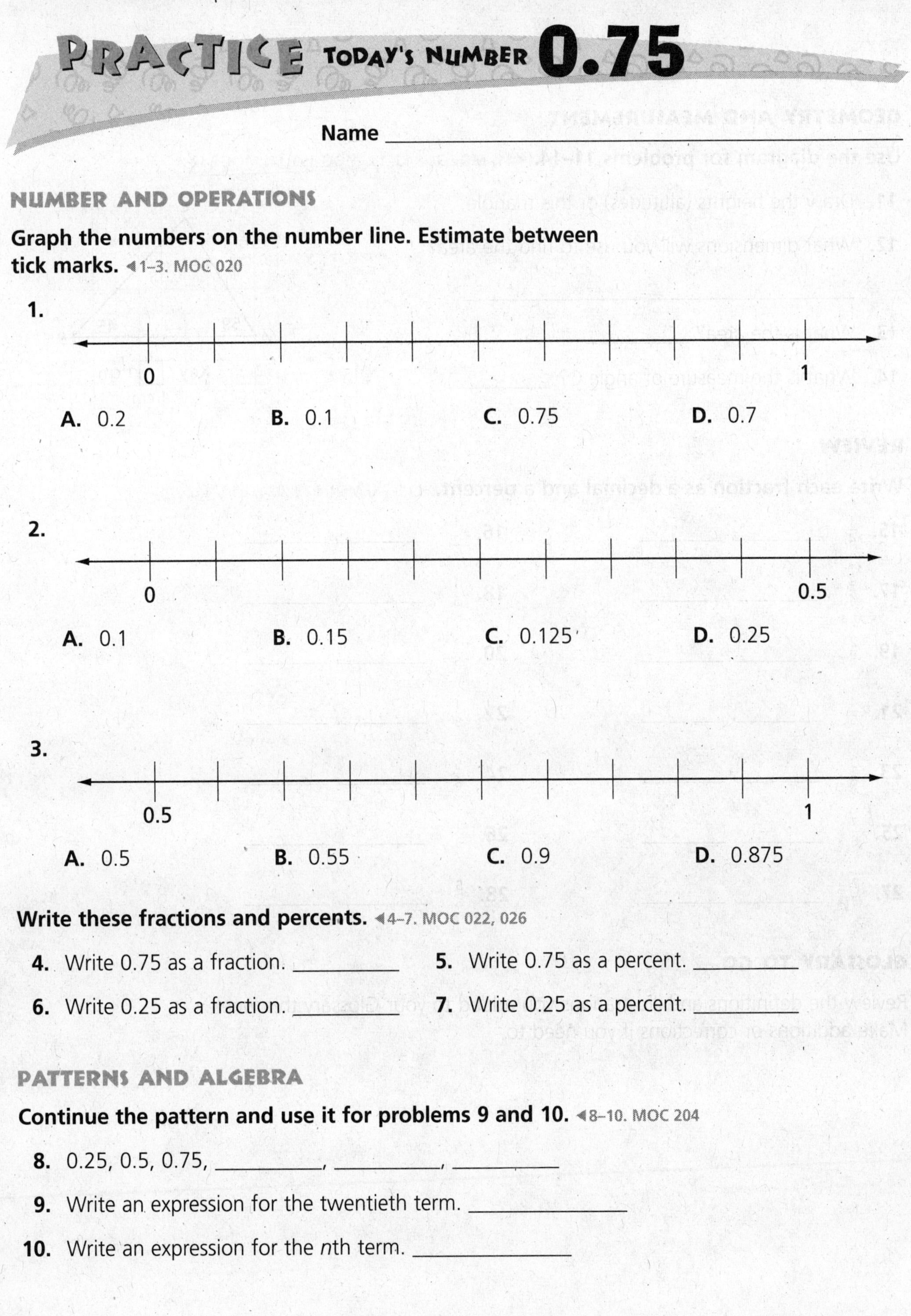

PRACTICE TODAY'S NUMBER 0.75

Name ______________________________

NUMBER AND OPERATIONS

Graph the numbers on the number line. Estimate between tick marks. ◀1–3. MOC 020

1.

0 1

A. 0.2 **B.** 0.1 **C.** 0.75 **D.** 0.7

2.

0 .... 0.5

A. 0.1 **B.** 0.15 **C.** 0.125 **D.** 0.25

3.

0.5 1

A. 0.5 **B.** 0.55 **C.** 0.9 **D.** 0.875

Write these fractions and percents. ◀4–7. MOC 022, 026

4. Write 0.75 as a fraction. __________

5. Write 0.75 as a percent. __________

6. Write 0.25 as a fraction. __________

7. Write 0.25 as a percent. __________

PATTERNS AND ALGEBRA

Continue the pattern and use it for problems 9 and 10. ◀8–10. MOC 204

8. 0.25, 0.5, 0.75, __________, __________, __________

9. Write an expression for the twentieth term. ______________

10. Write an expression for the *n*th term. ______________

GEOMETRY AND MEASUREMENT

Use the diagram for problems 11–14. ◄11. MOC 349 12–13. MOC 356 14. MOC 342

11. Draw the heights (altitudes) of this triangle.

12. What dimensions will you use to find the area?

____

13. What is the area? __________

14. What is the measure of angle C? __________

C
59°
45°
A
B
Key : 1 cm
1 cm

REVIEW

Write each fraction as a decimal and a percent. ◄15–28. MOC 023, 026, 044, 442

15. $\frac{1}{4}$ ________, ________

16. $\frac{1}{2}$ ________, ________

17. $\frac{3}{4}$ ________, ________

18. $\frac{1}{5}$ ________, ________

19. $\frac{2}{5}$ ________, ________

20. $\frac{3}{5}$ ________, ________

21. $\frac{4}{5}$ ________, ________

22. $\frac{1}{8}$ ________, ________

23. $\frac{3}{8}$ ________, ________

24. $\frac{5}{8}$ ________, ________

25. $\frac{7}{8}$ ________, ________

26. $\frac{1}{3}$ ________, ________

27. $\frac{2}{3}$ ________, ________

28. $\frac{5}{6}$ ________, ________

GLOSSARY TO GO

Review the definitions and illustrations you added to your Glossary this week. Make additions or corrections if you need to.

PROBLEM SOLVING

Name ______________________________

Problem Solving with Ratios: Rectangles

DIRECTIONS

- Rewrite the problem in your own words.
- Solve the problem. Circle the strategies you use.
- Show your work and complete the answer. Don't forget the units.

POSSIBLE STRATEGIES

- Guess, Check, and Revise
- Write an Equation
- Make a Model or a Diagram
- Other: ____________

PROBLEM 1

The perimeter of a rectangle is 70 centimeters. The width is 75% of the length. What are the dimensions of the rectangle?

The dimensions are: width ____________, and length ____________.

PROBLEM 2

The perimeter of a rectangle is 88 centimeters. The width is $\frac{1}{3}$ of the length. What are the dimensions of the rectangle?

The dimensions are: width ____________ , and length ____________.

ANALYZE YOUR WORK

1. Did your work on the first problem help you with the second problem? If so, how?

____

2. If you did not use the *Write an Equation* strategy, try to write one now for Problem 2.

____

NEWSLETTER

Summer Success: Math

Welcome to Summer Success Math! This week, the students have already reviewed many math skills

One part of the summer's work is to review computing with numbers for which students should not need paper and pencil or a calculator. We call this mental math and you can help your child sharpen this skill.

When you're out with your child, encourage the use of these mental math skills by working together to find prices for 10 items, for items on sale at a percent off, or for a 10% or 20% tip.

In class, we try always to read decimals as fractions. So, 1.6 is read *one and six tenths* instead of *one point six*. On the back of this page is a cross-number puzzle to reinforce this skill.

Enjoy your time with your child, and thank you for helping to strengthen your child's comfort with important math concepts.

NEWSLETTER

Reading Decimal Numbers

Use the clues to complete the puzzle. A decimal point fills a cell. The clue for 1 down is filled in for you.

		1 4	2	
3	4	1		5
6		0		
7		.		
	8	3		

Across

1. forty-one
3. two hundred sixty one and two tenths
6. one and forty-eight thousandths
7. fifty and fifty hundredths
8. twenty-three

Down

1. four hundred ten and three tenths
2. one and forty-five hundredths
3. two hundred fifteen
4. six and two hundredths
5. two hundred eighty

Enjoy these activities with your child. Remember that using math in the real world will help your child understand that math is important in school.

PRACTICE TODAY'S NUMBER 2^2

Name ______________________________

NUMBER AND OPERATIONS

Write the value of each exponential expression. ◄1–6. MOC 071

1. 2^3 __________ **2.** 3^2 __________

3. 4^2 __________ **4.** 12^2 __________

5. 15^2 __________ **6.** 100^2 __________

Write each expression in exponential form. ◄7–8. MOC 071

7. $2 \times 2 \times 2 \times 2 \times 2$ __________

8. $0.2 \times 0.2 \times 0.2$ __________

PATTERNS AND ALGEBRA

Put the numbers in order from least to greatest. ◄9–10. MOC 071

9. $2^3, 3^2, 1^{12}, 2^2$ ________, ________, ________, ________

10. $(\frac{1}{2})^4, (\frac{1}{2})^3, (\frac{1}{2})^{10}, (\frac{1}{2})^2$ ________, ________, ________, ________

Continue the pattern and use it for problem 12. ◄11–12. MOC 071

11. 2, 4, 8, 16, 32, ________, ________, ________

12. Describe how to find the twentieth term. ______________________

GEOMETRY AND MEASUREMENT

Draw the figure and use it in problem 14. ◄13. MOC 351–352 14. MOC 356

13. Use a ruler to sketch a right isosceles triangle with legs 30 millimeters long. Label the sides and angles you know.

14. Describe how to find the area of the triangle you drew.

____

____

REVIEW

Solve these problems. Show your work. ◀ 15. MOC 102 16–17. MOC 131 18. MOC 158–159 19. MOC 186

15. In a 3-day bike race, the bikers rode 80.52 kilometers on the first day, 50.58 kilometers on the second day, and 67.4 kilometers on the third day. How far did they ride?

____

16. How much heavier is a bike that weighs 12.64 kilograms than a bike that weighs 10.8 kilograms?

____

17. A major bicycle race covers 2,455 miles. In 2004, a German completed it in 100 hours, $30.58\overline{3}$ minutes. The French second-place competitor finished in 100 hours, $39.7\overline{3}$ minutes. By how many minutes, to the nearest hundredth, did the German win?

____

18. In another race, one biker rode at an average speed of 40.2 kilometer per hour. About how far had he traveled after 6 hours?

____

19. Another biker rode at an average speed of 45.1 kilometers per hour. If the biker rode 315.7 kilometers, about how many hours did she ride?

____

GLOSSARY TO GO

Write definitions and draw pictures illustrating new math terms. The vocabulary should be covered in your class time, so you should be familiar with most of the terms.

Make That Triangle

Object: Plot the vertices of 3 triangles that are as large as possible.

MATERIALS

Ruler, two 1 through 6 number cubes and two −1 through −6 number cubes, paper bag, pencils

DIRECTIONS

1. Write your name by one of the grids on the Coordinate Grids Game Board on page 34 of Player 2's book. Place the number cubes in the bag.
2. If you are Player 1, draw 2 number cubes from the bag. No peeking. After tossing the cubes, decide which number will be the *x*- and which the *y*-coordinate. After the first turn, **tell why** you made that decision. **(My first point is at (1, 2). I want to make it easy to find the length of the base, so I'll put my second point at (1, −4).)** Plot and label that point on your coordinate grid, then put the number cubes back in the bag.
3. Take turns until you have plotted 3 points. Carefully connect the points to make a triangle, then compute and record its area.
4. Make 3 triangles, then find the sum of their areas. If your sum is greater, you win.

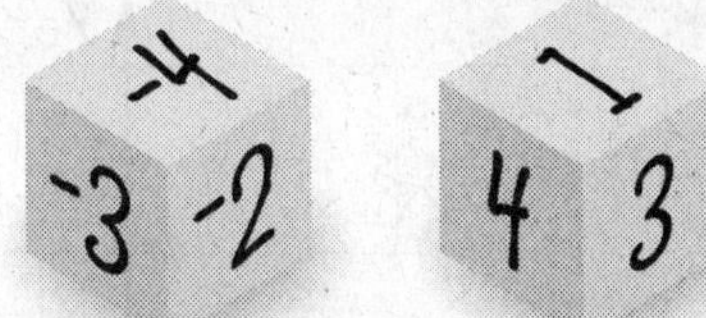

Coordinate Grid Game Board

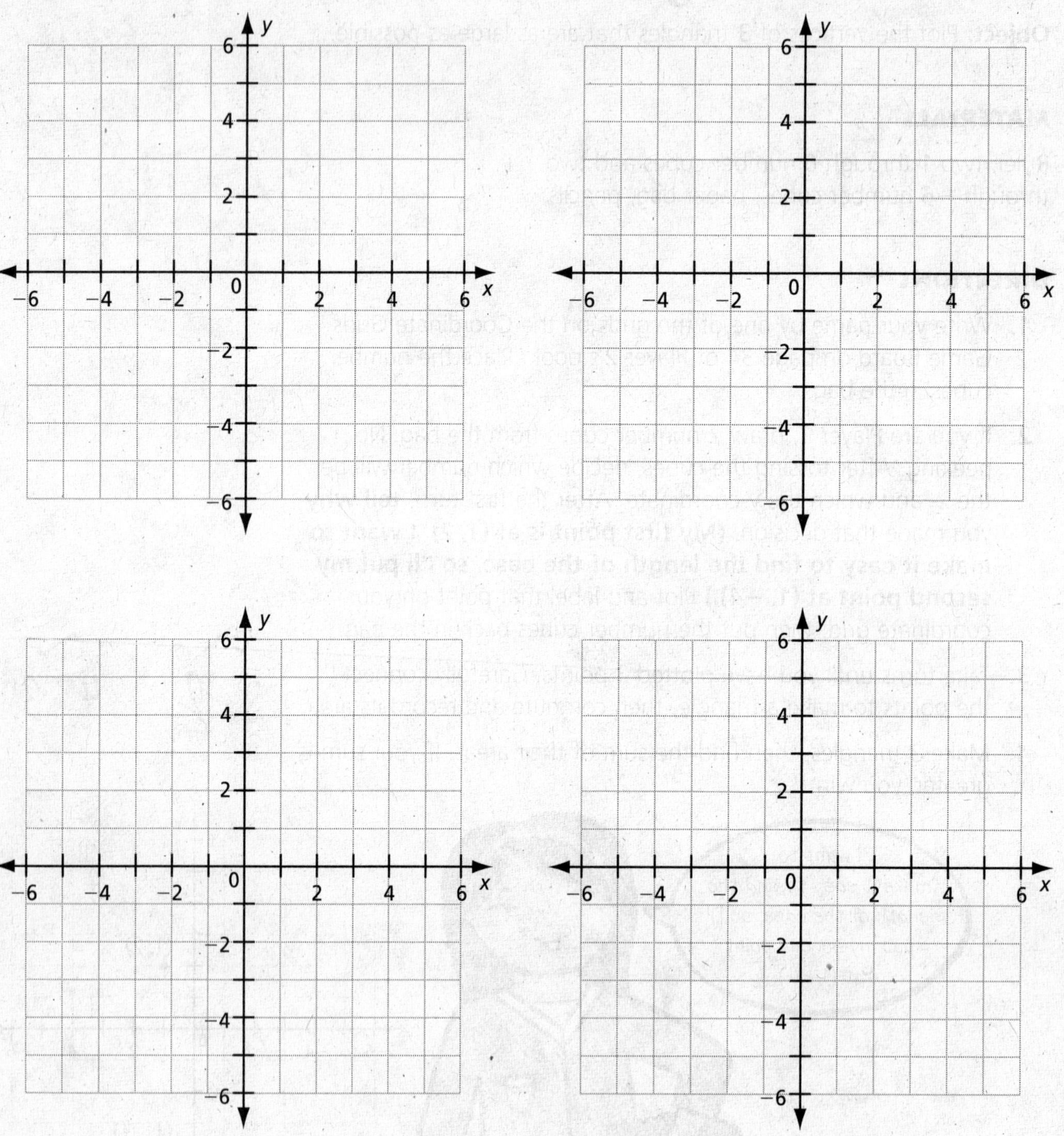

Name ______________________________

Making a Line Graph

How did running-shoe sales change throughout the year?

DIRECTIONS

- Work with a partner.
- Decide on the scale and interval for the line graph on page 36.
- Title your graph.
- Graph the data.
- Answer the questions to analyze the data.

Running-shoe Sales

Month	Pairs of Shoes Sold
January	16
February	28
March	34
April	39
May	46
June	38
July	36
August	32
September	29
October	20
November	16
December	26

ANALYZE THE DATA

1. Between which 2 months was the greatest increase in shoe sales? When was the greatest decrease?

   Greatest increase: ______________________________

   Greatest decrease: ______________________________

2. Describe any trends you see in the data. You may want to consider time periods where shoe sales were increasing or decreasing.

   ____
   ____
   ____

3. Was there any month when the data did not fit a trend? Explain why you think that occurred.

   ____
   ____
   ____

Making a Line Graph

Title: ______________________________

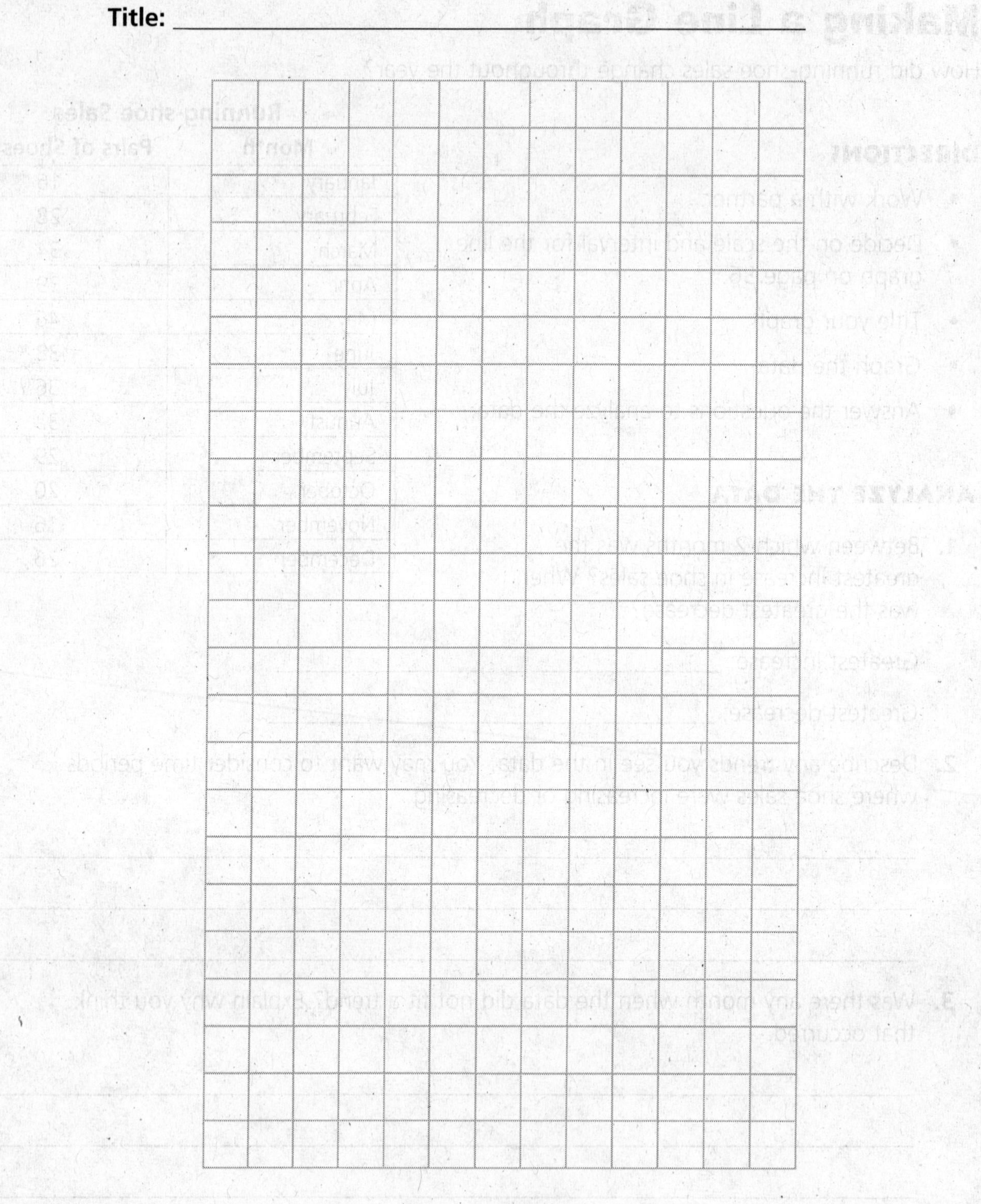

PRACTICE TODAY'S NUMBER 3^3

Name ______________________

NUMBER AND OPERATIONS

Write the value of each expression. ◂1–6. MOC 080

1. 3^3 __________ **2.** 4^3 __________ **3.** 5^3 __________

4. 6^3 __________ **5.** 10^3 __________ **6.** 100^3 __________

PATTERNS AND ALGEBRA

Continue the pattern and answer the related question. ◂7–8. MOC 071

7. 3, 9, 27, 81, __________, __________

8. If the pattern above continues, how can you find the fifteenth term? __________

GEOMETRY AND MEASUREMENT

Draw the figure and answer the related question. ◂9–10. MOC 332–335

9. Draw a pair of supplementary angles. Label both angles using one variable to show how they're related.

10. Describe the difference between supplementary and complementary angles.

____

____

Write the volume of each cube. ◂11–14. MOC 080

11. 3 cm

$V =$ __________

12. $\frac{1}{2}$ in.

$V =$ __________

13. 0.5 m

$V =$ __________

14. n units

$V =$ __________

REVIEW

Complete the table. ◂15. MOC 071

15. There is an old story about a king who promised his faithful servant a grain of rice on the first day, 2 grains of rice on the second day, 4 grains of rice on the third day, and double the number of grains on each succeeding day. Fill in this table to show the number of grains of rice the servant received each day for the first 12 days. The first 3 days have been done for you.

Day	Grains of Rice	Exponential Expression
1	1	2^0
2	2	2^1
3	4	2^2
4	8	
5		
6		
7		
8		
9		
10		
11		
12		

GLOSSARY TO GO

Write definitions and draw pictures illustrating new math terms. The vocabulary should be covered in your class time, so you should be familiar with most of the terms.

DATA STUDY

Name ______________________________

Making a Histogram and a Circle Graph

How did shoe sales vary over the year?

DIRECTIONS

- Work with a partner.
- Decide on the scale and intervals for the histogram on the next page.
- Calculate the number of pairs of shoes sold in each quarter of the year.
- Complete and title both of your data displays.
- Write a key that explains how to read the circle graph.
- Answer the questions to analyze the data.

Running Shoe Sales

Month	Pairs of Shoes Sold
January	16
February	28
March	34
April	39
May	46
June	38
July	36
August	32
September	29
October	20
November	16
December	26

ANALYZE THE DATA

1. For which interval on the histogram is there the greatest frequency? Where is the least frequency?

Greatest frequency: ____________

Least frequency: ____________

2. Explain how to use the circle graph to find the quarter in which the most running shoes sold and how that amount compares to the total year's sales.

____

____

____

3. Compare your histogram and circle graph with the line graph of the same data from page 36. What are the benefits of using each type of display?

____

____

____

Making a Histogram and a Circle Graph

Title ______________________________

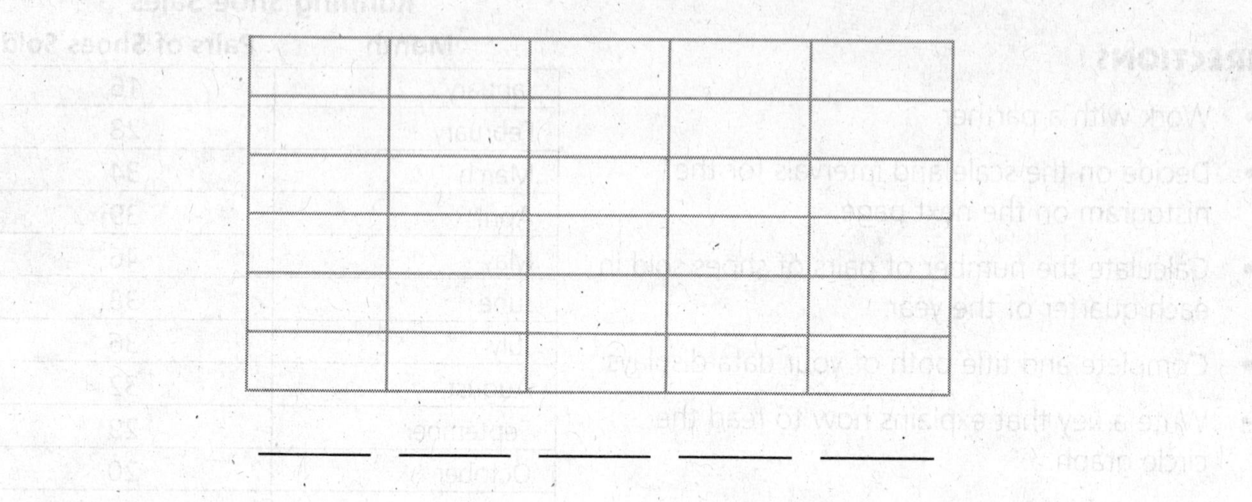

Title ______________________________

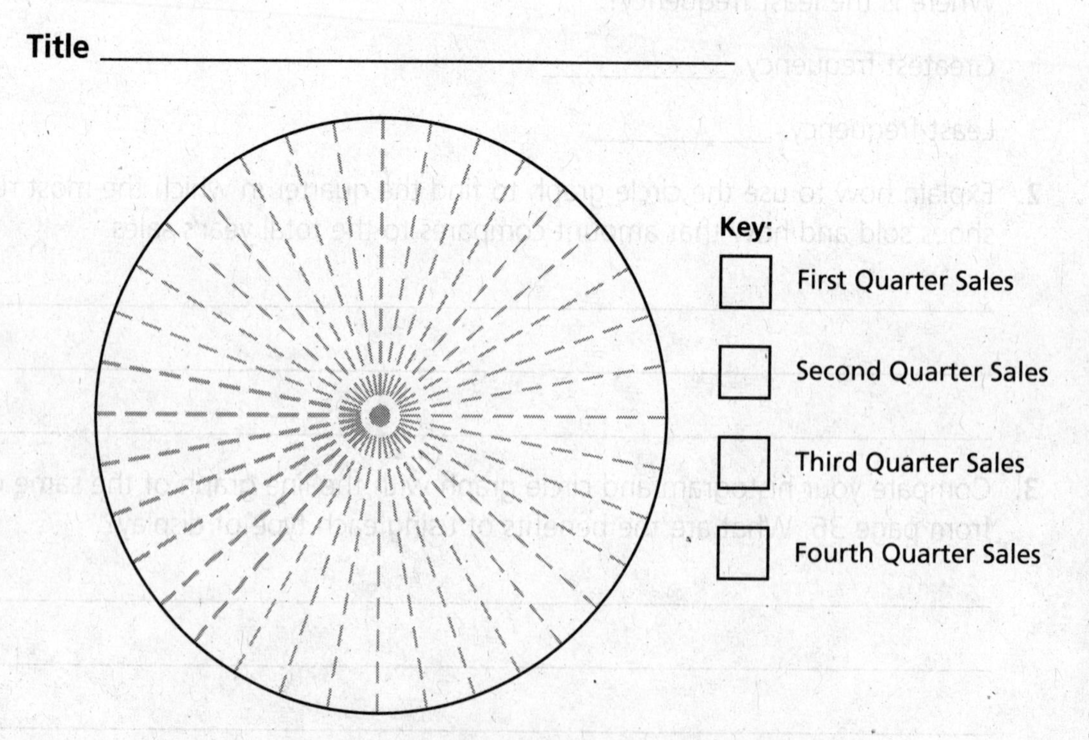

PRACTICE TODAY'S NUMBER 10^3

Name ______________________

NUMBER AND OPERATIONS

Write each product as a power of 10. ◀ 1–3. MOC 071

1. $10^3 \times 10^3$ ______ **2.** $10^2 \times 10^6$ ______ **3.** $10^5 \times 10^5$ ______

Write each product as an exponential expression. ◀ 4–6. MOC 071

4. $2^4 \times 2^2$ ______ **5.** $3^2 \times 3^3$ ______ **6.** $5^2 \times 5^2$ ______

PATTERNS AND ALGEBRA

Solve the problem. ◀ 7–8. MOC 080

7. What is the length of an edge of a cube that has a volume of 125 cubic centimeters?

______

8. How can you estimate the length of the edge of a cube if its volume is not a perfect cube?

____

____

GEOMETRY AND MEASUREMENT

Write the area of each triangle. ◀ 9–11. MOC 356

9.

$A =$ ______

10.

$A =$ ______

11.

$A =$ ______

Draw the figure and answer the related question. ◀12. MOC 351–353 13. MOC 376,

12. Draw and label an equilateral triangle, a right scalene triangle, an acute isosceles triangle, and an obtuse scalene triangle.

13. Explain how you know that one of your triangles is similar to one from any other student in the class.

____

____

REVIEW

Complete the table. ◀14. MOC 071

14. Which would give you more money, earning $1,000 a day for 15 days, or earning $1 on the first day, $2 on the second day, $4 on the third day, and so on, doubling each day? Fill in the table to help you decide.

____

Day	Dollars	Total Dollars
1	1	1
2	2	3
3	4	7
4	8	
5		
6		
7		
8		
9		
10		
11		
12		
13		
14		
15		

GLOSSARY TO GO

Write definitions and draw pictures illustrating new math terms. The vocabulary should be covered in your class time, so you should be familiar with most of the terms.

More or Less

Object: Fill the blanks with percents in order from least to greatest.

MATERIALS

Two 1–6 number cubes, paper, pencils

DIRECTIONS

1. Make a recording sheet with 3 spaces between 0% and 50%, 3 spaces between 50% and 100%, and 3 spaces after 100%.
2. If you are Player 1, roll both number cubes and use the digits to make a fraction. Use mental math to find the equivalent percent. Write the percent in one of the blanks on your recording sheet. **Explain why** you chose the fraction you did. **(I can make $\frac{2}{3}$ or $\frac{3}{2}$. I think I'll use $\frac{2}{3}$ so I don't group my percents too close together.)**
3. Once a space has been used, it cannot be changed, and you cannot use the same number more than once. So, you cannot use 50% or 100%.
4. If you can't place a percent in the correct order, your turn is over.
5. Take turns rolling the cubes, making a fraction, and finding the percent. If you are first to fill the 9 spaces on your recording sheet, you win.

Name Charlette

0% ______ ______ ______ 50% $66\frac{2}{3}$% ______ ______ 100% ______ 200% ______

PROBLEM SOLVING

Name ______________________________

Problem Solving: Patterns in Squares

DIRECTIONS

- Solve the problem. Circle the strategies you use.
- Show your work. Don't forget the units.

POSSIBLE STRATEGIES

- Make a Model or a Diagram
- Make a Table or an Organized List
- Write an Equation
- Other: __________

Figure 1 **Figure 2** **Figure 3** **Figure 4**

PROBLEM 1

A. Draw Figure 4.

B. What is the area of each shaded square?

____

C. What is the area of each entire square?

____

PROBLEM 2 Use your work in Problem 1.

A. If the area of a shaded square is 49 square units, what is the Figure number? ________

B. If the area of the whole square is 196 square units, what is the Figure number? ________

ANALYZE YOUR WORK

1. Describe the general pattern.

____

____

2. If you did not use the *Write an Equation* strategy, try to write one for the area of a shaded square and one for the area of a whole square.

____

____

Name ____________________

NUMBER AND OPERATIONS

Write each product in exponential form. Then write its value. ◀1–3. MOC 071, 162

1. $2^3 \times 2^4$ ____________ **2.** $\left(\frac{1}{2}\right)^3 \times \left(\frac{1}{2}\right)^2$ ____________ **3.** $\left(\frac{1}{2}\right)^3 \times \left(\frac{1}{2}\right)^3$ ____________

Write each quotient in exponential form. Then write its value. ◀4–6. MOC 071, 187–191

4. $2^6 \div 2^4$ ____________ **5.** $\left(\frac{1}{2}\right)^4 \div \left(\frac{1}{2}\right)^2$ ____________ **6.** $\left(\frac{1}{2}\right)^4 \div \left(\frac{1}{2}\right)^3$ ____________

PATTERNS AND ALGEBRA

Write the rule. ◀7–8. MOC 071

7. Describe how to find the product of 2 exponential expressions with the same base.

____

8. Describe how to find the quotient of 2 exponential expressions with the same base.

____

GEOMETRY AND MEASUREMENT

Use the diagram to answer the questions. ◀9–11. MOC 356, 376

9. How can you tell that these triangles are similar?

____

____

____

____

53°
10 cm
6 cm
8 cm
Triangle A

53°
5 cm
3 cm
4 cm
Triangle B

10. What is the area of Triangle A? ____________

11. What is the ratio of the area of the Triangle B to the area of Triangle A? ________

REVIEW

Write each product as a power of 10. Then write its value. ◀12–23. MOC 071

12. $10^1 \times 10^1$ ____________________

13. $10^1 \times 10^2$ ____________________

14. $10^1 \times 10^3$ ____________________

15. $10^2 \times 10^2$ ____________________

16. $10^2 \times 10^3$ ____________________

17. $10^2 \times 10^4$ ____________________

18. $10^3 \times 10^3$ ____________________

19. $10^3 \times 10^4$ ____________________

20. $10^3 \times 10^5$ ____________________

21. $10^3 \times 10^6$ ____________________

22. What pattern do you see between the exponents in each problem and the exponent in its answer?

____

23. What pattern do you see between the exponent in each answer and the number of zeros in its value?

____

GLOSSARY TO GO

Write definitions and draw pictures illustrating new math terms. The vocabulary should be covered in your class time, so you should be familiar with most of the terms.

Name ______________________________

Problem Solving: Patterns in Cubes

DIRECTIONS

- Rewrite the problem in your own words.
- Solve the problem. Circle the strategies you use.
- Show your work.

POSSIBLE STRATEGIES

- Guess, Check, and Revise
- Make a Model or a Diagram
- Other: ____________

PROBLEM 1

Twenty-seven cubes fill a box that is also a cube. Fill in the blanks.

A. ________ cubes touch the bottom.

B. ________ cubes touch the lid.

C. ________ cubes touch the sides.

D. ________ cube doesn't touch the box.

PROBLEM 2

One thousand cubes fill a box that is also a cube. Fill in the blanks.

A. ________ cubes touch the bottom.

B. ________ cubes touch the lid.

C. ________ cubes touch the sides.

D. ________ cubes don't touch the box.

ANALYZE YOUR WORK

1. Did your work on the first problem help you with the second problem? If so, how?

____

2. Is there anything you did while working on either problem that made it easier for you to solve the problem? If so, what was it? If not, can you think of something now that might have helped?

____

PRACTICE TODAY'S NUMBER n^2

Name ______________________

NUMBER AND OPERATIONS

Write each expression in exponential form. ◀1–2. MOC 071

1. $10 \times 10 \times 10 \times 10$ ________

2. $n \times n \times n \times n$ ________

Write each product in exponential form. ◀3–5. MOC 071

3. $2^2 \times 2^2$ ________

4. $10^4 \times 10^2$ ________

5. $n^4 \times n^3$ ________

Write each quotient in exponential form. ◀6–8. MOC 071

6. $2^4 \div 2^2$ ________

7. $10^7 \div 10^6$ ________

8. $n^5 \div n^2$ ________

PATTERNS AND ALGEBRA

Fill in the blank. ◀9–12. MOC 071, 160–162

9. If $n = \frac{1}{2}$, then $n^2 =$ ________

10. If $n = 100$, then $n^2 =$ ________

11. Does $3^2 \times 2^2 = 5^2$? Explain.

____

____

12. Does $n^2 + n^2 = n^4$? Explain why or why not?

____

____

GEOMETRY AND MEASUREMENT

Use the diagram to answer the questions. ◀13. MOC 334, 342–343 14. MOC 376

13. What is the measure of angle B? ________

14. These triangles are similar. How can you find the length of side EF?

B
2 in.
60°
120°
A
C
E
4 in.
D
F

____

____

REVIEW

Fill in the blanks as quickly as possible using mental math. ◀15–18. MOC 158; 19–22. MOC 161; 23–27. MOC 442–445

15. 0.75 of 4 = ________

16. 0.75 of 8 = ________

17. 0.75 of 12 = ________

18. 0.75 of 16 = ________

19. $\frac{3}{4}$ of 40 = ________

20. $\frac{3}{4}$ of 80 = ________

21. $\frac{3}{4}$ of 120 = ________

22. $\frac{3}{4}$ of 160 = ________

23. 75% of 400 = ________

24. 75% of 800 = ________

25. 75% of 1,200 = ________

26. 75% of 1,600 = ________

27. A CD is on sale for 75% of the original price. It costs $12 on sale. What was the original price of the CD?

____

GLOSSARY TO GO

Review the definitions and illustrations you added to your Glossary this week. Make additions or corrections if you need to.

Name ______________________________

Problem Solving: Perfect Square Sums

DIRECTIONS

- Solve the problem. Circle the strategies you use.
- Show your work.

POSSIBLE STRATEGIES

- Guess, Check, and Revise
- Make an Organized List
- Other: ____________

PROBLEM 1

Arrange the numbers 5, 7, 18, 29, 31 in a row so that the sum of any 2 adjacent numbers is a perfect square.

_____ _____ _____ _____ _____

PROBLEM 2

Arrange the numbers 1 through 15 in a row so that the sum of any 2 adjacent numbers is a perfect square.

_____ _____ _____ _____ _____ _____ _____ _____ _____ _____ _____ _____ _____ _____ _____

ANALYZE YOUR WORK

1. Did your work on the first problem help you with the second problem? If so, how?

____

2. Is there anything you did while working on either problem that made it easier for you to solve the problem? If so, what was it? If not, can you think of something now that might have helped?

____

Summer Success: Math

This week, we worked with exponents. An exponent is a number that is used to tell how many times to use another number as a factor. Together, the exponent and its base (the factor) are called an exponential expression.

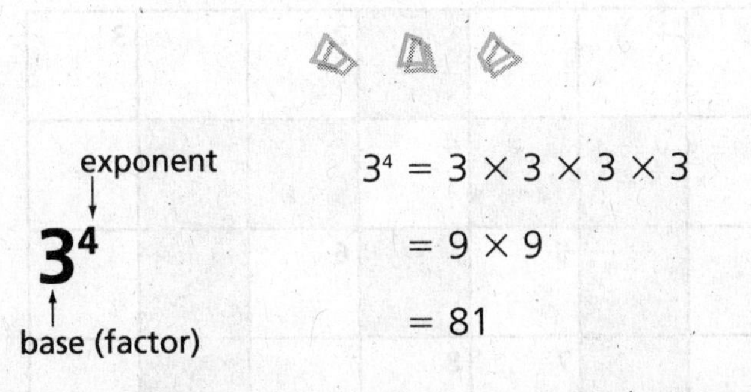

Many exponential expressions come up over and over again and your child will be practicing using mental math to find their values. You can help by asking questions like these.

- These floor tiles are 3-inch squares. What is the area of one tile? (9 square inches) How many tiles will fit in this 1-yard square part of the kitchen? (144)
- This bag of potting soil says it contains 3 cubic feet. How many of these 1 foot × 1 foot × 1 foot planters can I fill with a bag? (3)
- Will you read the label on that can of paint and help me figure out whether it will cover the wall in the living room?

On the back of this page is a cross-number puzzle using some of this week's skills. Ask your child to show you how to solve it.

Enjoy your time with your child, and thank you for helping to strengthen your child's comfort with important math concepts.

NEWSLETTER

Writing and Evaluating Exponential Expressions

Use the clues to complete the puzzle.

1				2		3
			4			
		5		6		
		7	8			
	9					

Across

1. 10^2

2. $2^2 \times 10^2 + 2$

4. 2^2

7. $5^2 \times 10$

9. 10^4

Down

1. 10^3

3. 2×10^3

5. $3^2 \times 2^3 \times 10$

6. $3^2 \times 10^2$

8. $5^2 \times 2$

Show your child that you're proud of his or her progress. Remember that using math in the real world will help your child understand that math is important in school.

PRACTICE TODAY'S NUMBER −20

Name ______________________

NUMBER AND OPERATIONS

Write the opposite of each integer. ◂1–4. MOC 046–047

1. −15 ________ **2.** 4 ________

3. 18 ________ **4.** −7 ________

Write each absolute value. ◂5–8. MOC 050–051

5. |−12| ________ **6.** |8| ________

7. |0| ________ **8.** |−5| ________

Add the integers. ◂9–12. MOC 108

9. −20 + 20 = ________ **10.** 15 + (−25) = ________

11. −20 + (−20) = ________ **12.** 15 + (−10) = ________

Solve the problems. Show your work. ◂13. MOC 108; 14. MOC 164

13. If a football team gains 15 yards on one play and then loses 5 yards on the next play, what is the total number of yards gained?

____

14. A football team lost 12 yards four times in a row. Write a multiplication fact using integers to show the action.

____

PATTERNS AND ALGEBRA

Continue the pattern and answer the related question. ◂15–16. MOC 108

15. 14, 11, 8, ________, ________, ________, ________

16. What number is added to each term to get the next term? ________

GEOMETRY AND MEASUREMENT

Draw the figure and answer the related question. ◂17. MOC 318–320, 351–353; 18. MOC 356

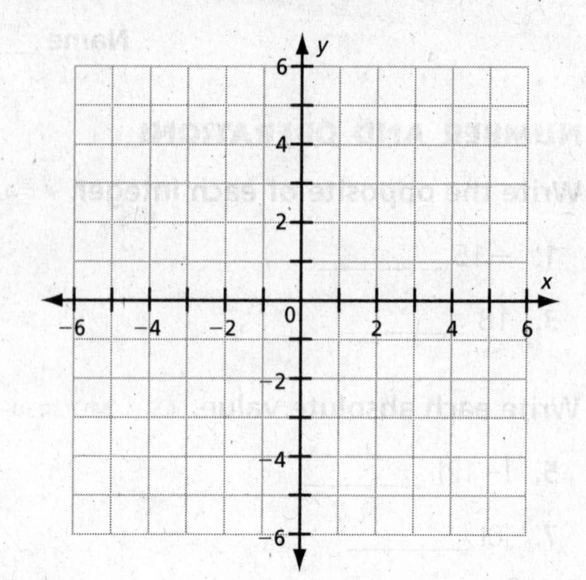

17. Plot points (4, 0), (−4, 0), and (0, −6). Then connect them in order. What is the name of the shape? Be as specific as possible.

____

18. What is the area of this figure?

____

REVIEW

Solve the problems. ◂19–22. MOC 442–445

19. In softball, a batting average is the ratio of the number of hits a batter gets to the number of times at bat. If a player hits the ball 12 times out of 32 times at bat, what is his batting average?

____

20. A teammate has a batting average of 0.625, or 62.5%. She had 24 times at bat. How many hits did she get? Show your work.

____

21. The softball trophies were bought on sale at 20% off. Each one cost $6.40. What was the original price? Show your work.

____

22. If the coaches bought 12 trophies at the sale price in problem 21, how much did they save altogether?

____

GLOSSARY TO GO

Write definitions and draw pictures illustrating new math terms. The vocabulary should be covered in your class time, so you should be familiar with most of the terms.

GAME

Plot a Quadrilateral

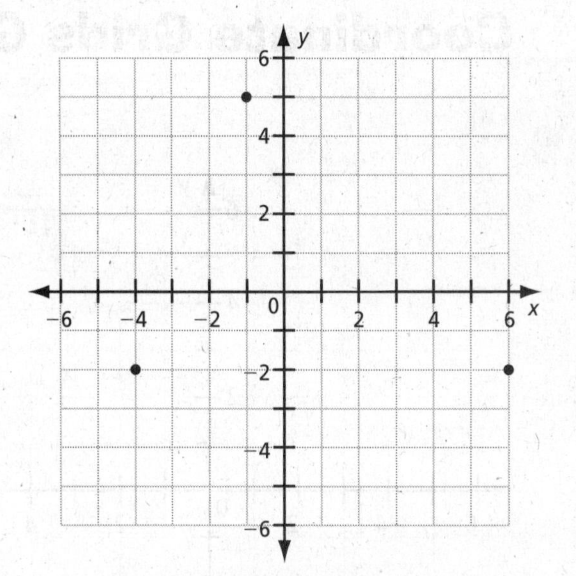

Object: Plot the vertices of large quadrilaterals. Bonus points are awarded for congruent and parallel sides.

MATERIALS

Two 1 through 6 number cubes, two −1 through −6 number cubes, paper bag, pencils, paper

DIRECTIONS

1. Use the Coordinate Grids Game Boards in Player 1's book. If you are Player 1, use the grids on the left. If you are Player 2, use the grids on the right. Make a recording sheet like the one below.
2. Place the number cubes in the paper bag. Draw 2 number cubes from the bag. No peeking. After rolling the cubes, decide which number will be the *x*- and which the *y*-coordinate. **Tell why** you made your decision. **(If I use point (3, 5), I will have a pair of parallel sides.)** Plot and label that point on your first grid, then return the cubes to the bag.
3. Take turns until both of you have plotted 4 points. Connect your points to make a quadrilateral. Find and record its area.
4. Your score is the number of square units of area in your quadrilateral plus 5 points for each pair of congruent or parallel sides.
5. After 2 rounds, add your points. The higher score wins.

	Player Number	Area	Pairs of Parallel Sides x 5	Pairs of Congruent Sides x 5	Total Points
Round 1	1				
	2				
Round 2	1				
	2				

Coordinate Grids Game Board

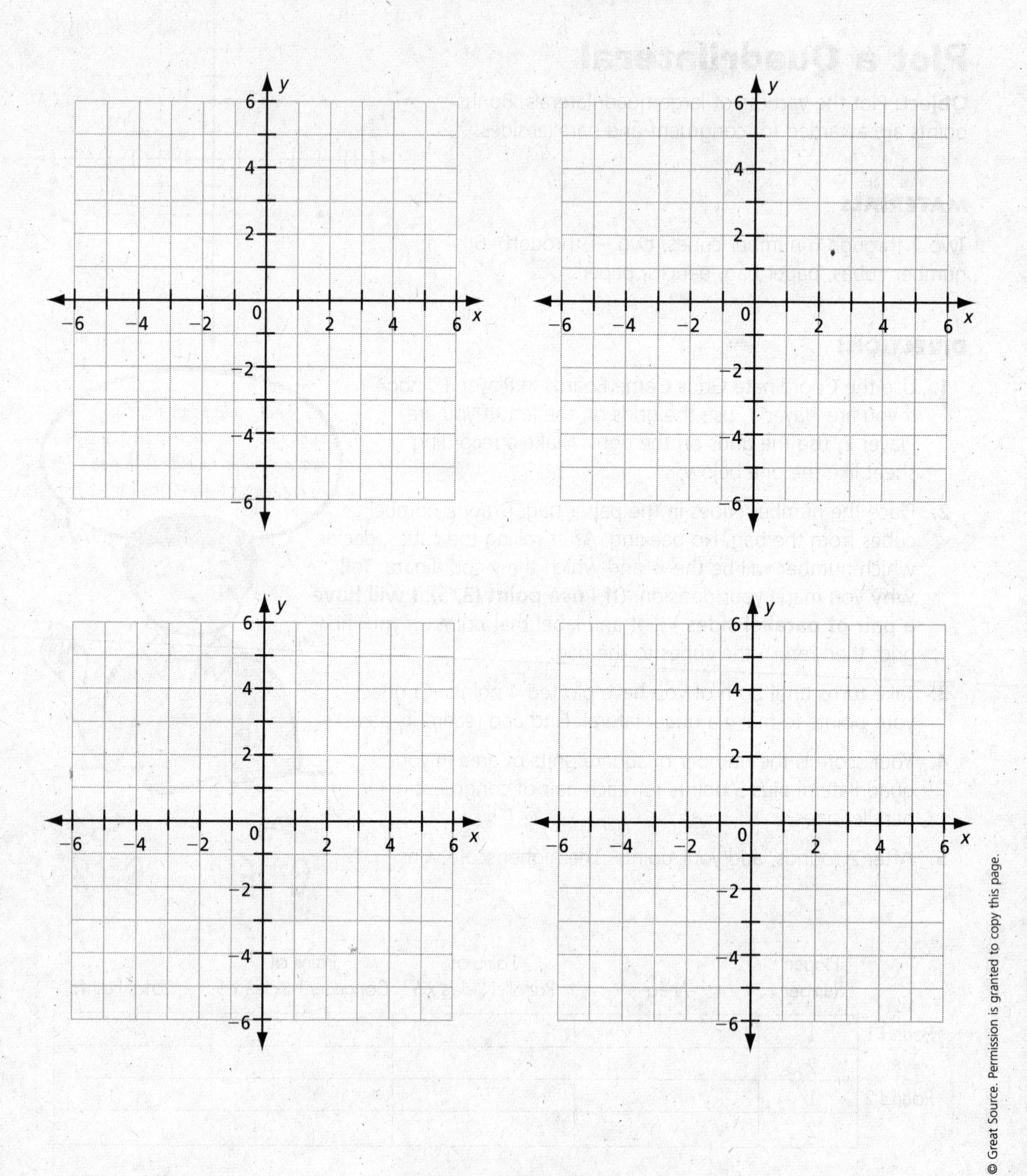

Name ______________________________

Making a Box-and-Whisker Plot

How much variation is there in the amount of monthly precipitation in Orlando, Florida?

DIRECTIONS

- Work with a partner.
- Write the precipitation data for Orlando in order from least to greatest on page 60.
- Find the upper and lower extremes in the data.
- Find the median for the full set of data.
- Find the median for the upper and lower halves of data.
- Title your plot and plot the data.
- Answer the questions to analyze the data.

Average Monthly Precipitation in Inches

City	Jan	Feb	Mar	Apr	May	June	July	Aug	Sept	Oct	Nov	Dec
Orlando, FL	2.4	2.4	3.5	2.4	3.7	7.4	7.2	6.3	5.8	2.7	2.3	2.3
Seattle, WA	5.1	4.2	3.8	2.6	1.8	1.5	0.8	1.0	1.6	3.2	5.9	5.6

Source: Weather.com

ANALYZE THE DATA

1. Find the mean precipitation for Orlando to the nearest tenth of an inch. How does the mean compare to the median value in the plot?

____

____

2. Write 2 facts about the data that you can see from the box-and-whisker plot.

____

____

Making a Box-and-Whisker Plot

Ordered Orlando data:

____

____

____

____

____

____

____

____

____

____

____

____

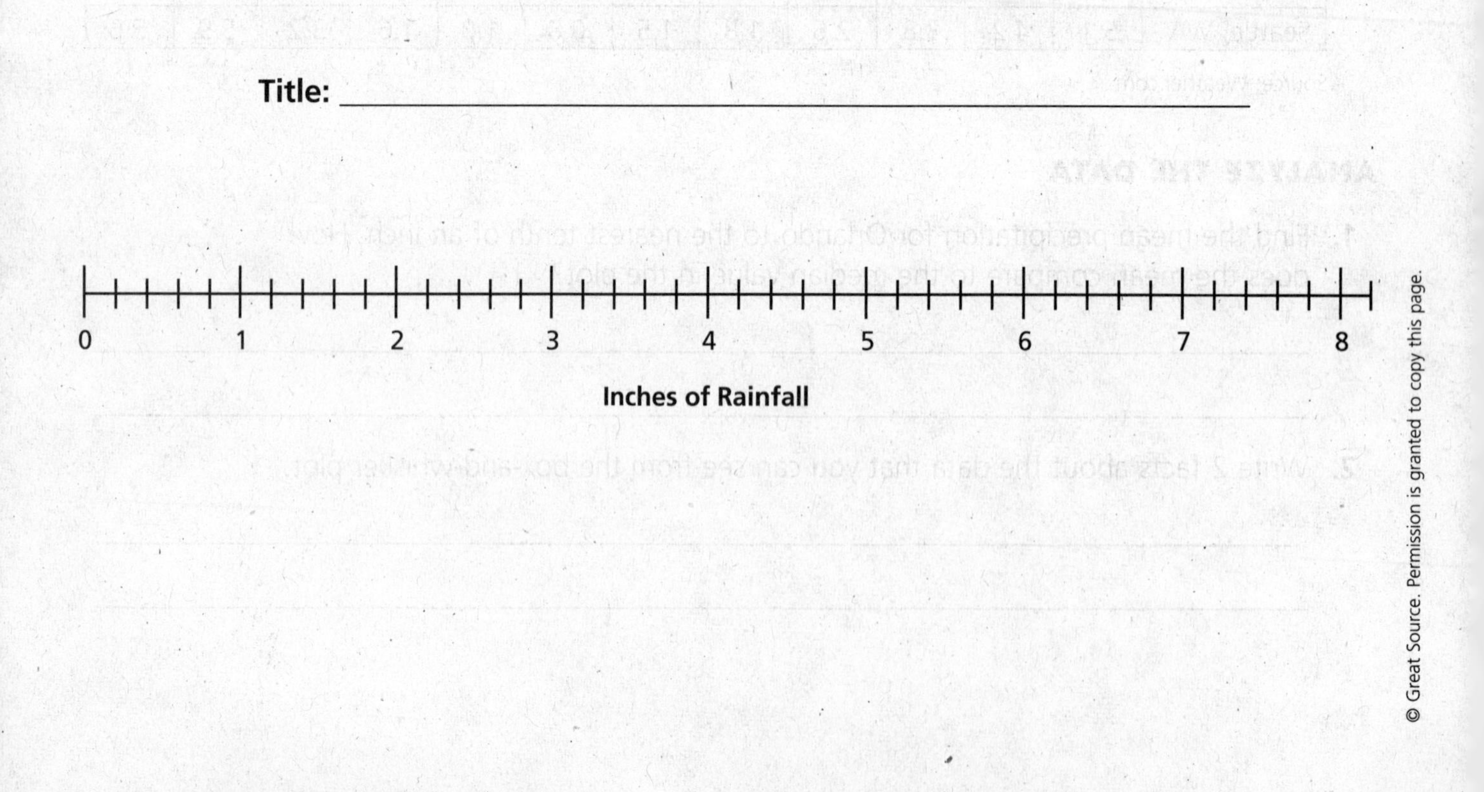

PRACTICE TODAY'S NUMBER −25

Name ______________________

NUMBER AND OPERATIONS

Answer each question. ◀1–2. MOC 056 3–4. MOC 046–051

1. What are the factors of 25? ______________

2. Name one pair of factors of −25.

____

3. $|-25|$ ________

4. What is the opposite of 25? ________

Write each sum. ◀5–6. MOC 108

5. $-25 + (-25) =$ ________

6. $-25 + 25 =$ ________

Write each difference. ◀7–12. MOC 136

7. $-25 - 20 =$ ________

8. $-25 - (-20) =$ ________

9. $-25 - 25 =$ ________

10. $25 - (-10) =$ ________

11. $10 - (-25) =$ ________

12. $10 - 25 =$ ________

PATTERNS AND ALGEBRA

Solve the problems. Look for a pattern. ◀13–15. MOC 108, 136

13. $3 + (-5) + 6 + (-8) + 9 + (-11) =$ ________

14. $-2 + 2 + (-3) + 3 =$ ________

15. Write a rule for subtracting integers. Then give 4 different examples using one number and its opposite.

____

____

GEOMETRY

Draw the figure and answer the related questions. ◀16. MOC 318–320, 351–353
17. MOC 386 18. MOC 389

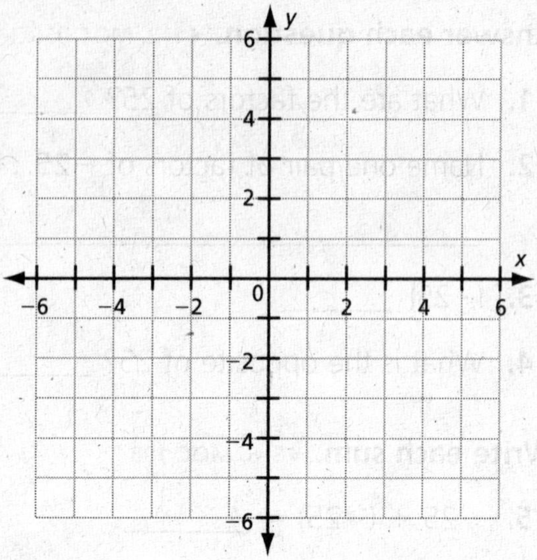

16. Plot points (−1, 2), (0, 6), and (4, −2). Then connect them in order. What kind of figure have you drawn? Be as specific as possible.

____

17. If you rotate the shape, will it rotate onto itself before turning 360°?

____

18. How many lines of symmetry does the shape have?

____

REVIEW

Solve the problems. ◀19–28. MOC 108, 136

19. −20 + (−20) = ________

20. −20 + 20 = ________

21. 20 + (−20) = ________

22. 20 + 20 = ________

23. How far is it from −36 to −36? ________

24. −36 − 36 = ________

25. −36 − (−36) = ________

26. 36 − (−36) = ________

27. 36 − 36 = ________

28. What patterns do you notice about the addition and subtraction of integers?

____

____

____

____

____

GLOSSARY TO GO

Write definitions and draw pictures illustrating new math terms. The vocabulary should be covered in your class time, so you should be familiar with most of the terms.

Name ______________________________

Comparing Box-and-Whisker Plots

How do the amounts of monthly precipitation compare for Orlando and Seattle?

DIRECTIONS

- Work with a partner.
- Use the Seattle data to make a box-and-whisker plot on page 64.
- Answer the questions to analyze the data.

Average Monthly Precipitation in Inches

City	Jan	Feb	Mar	Apr	May	June	July	Aug	Sept	Oct	Nov	Dec
Orlando, FL	2.4	2.4	3.5	2.4	3.7	7.4	7.2	6.3	5.8	2.7	2.3	2.3
Seattle, WA	5.1	4.2	3.8	2.6	1.8	1.5	0.8	1.0	1.6	3.2	5.9	5.6

Source: Weather.com

ANALYZE THE DATA

1. Compare the range of monthly rainfall averages for both cities.

____

____

2. How does the median precipitation for Seattle compare to that of Orlando?

____

____

3. Compare the box-and-whisker plots for each city. Tell how the plots and the data are similar, and how they are different.

____

____

____

Comparing Box-and-Whisker Plots

Ordered Seattle data:

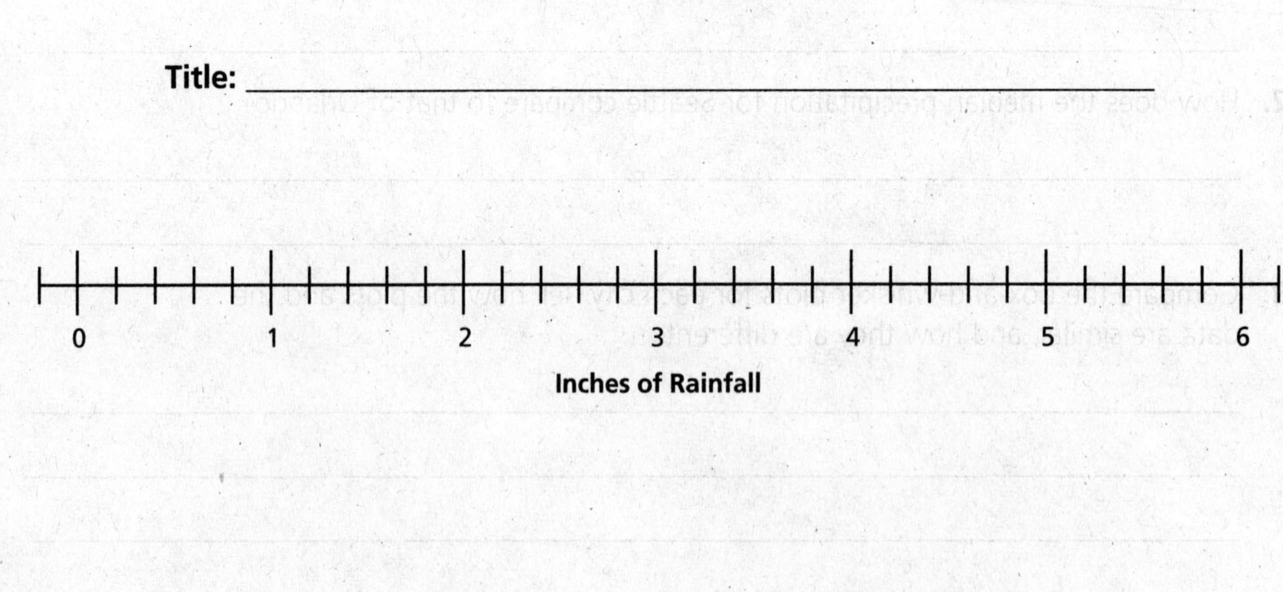

PRACTICE TODAY'S NUMBER −60

Name ______________________________

NUMBER AND OPERATIONS

Solve. ◂1. MOC 046–047; 2. 050–051; 3. 056, 164

1. What is the opposite of −60? ________

2. |−60| = ________

3. Write a pair of factors of −60.

____

____

Write each missing number. ◂4–11. MOC 164

4. 3 × (−20) = ________

5. −3 × (−20) = ________

6. 3 × 20 = ________

7. −3 × 20 = ________

8. 3 × ________ = 60

9. −5 × ________ = −60

10. ________ × 15 = −60

11. ________ × 10 = −60

Study problems 4–11 to help with problem 12. ◂12. MOC 164

12. Write some rules for multiplying integers.

____

____

PATTERNS AND ALGEBRA

Find *n*. ◂13–16. MOC 108, 136

13. $n - 20 = -60$; $n =$ ________

14. $n + (-20) = 60$; $n =$ ________

15. $60 - n = -10$; $n =$ ________

16. $n - (-1) = -60$; n ________

GEOMETRY AND MEASUREMENT

Draw the polygon and answer the related questions. ◂17. MOC 318–320, 363; 18. MOC 368; 19. MOC 389

17. Draw a coordinate grid and plot the points $(-2, 2)$, $(1, 4)$, $(1, -3)$, and $(-2, -1)$. Then connect them in order. What is the name of this polygon?

____

18. What is the area of this polygon?

____

19. Mark any lines of symmetry on the diagram.

REVIEW

Answer each question. ◂20–25. MOC 107, 135

20. A recipe calls for combining $\frac{3}{8}$ cup of milk and $\frac{3}{4}$ cup of water, and then adding one third of that mixture to a cup of flour. How much liquid is added to the flour?

____

21. $1\frac{1}{4} + 2\frac{1}{3} + 1\frac{3}{4} + 3\frac{2}{3} =$ ________

22. $1\frac{3}{8} + 2\frac{1}{4} + \frac{3}{8} =$ ________

23. If $n + \frac{1}{2} = 1\frac{3}{4}$, $n =$ ________

24. If $n - \frac{3}{4} = 1\frac{3}{8}$, $n =$ ________

25. Complete the table so that the sum of all the rows, columns, and diagonals is $\frac{15}{3}$, or 5.

$\frac{2}{3}$		$\frac{6}{3}$
$\frac{9}{3}$		
		$\frac{8}{3}$

GLOSSARY TO GO

Write definitions and draw pictures illustrating new math terms. The vocabulary should be covered in your class time, so you should be familiar with most of the terms.

GAME

Integer Sums

Object: Find 4 integer sums in a row on the Game Board.

-2	5	-7	8	6	-1
1	0	-4	10	-9	-7
-10	4	3	-5	-3	9
5	8	-6	1	2	-3
-4	-1	-7	-8	7	0
-6	-5	2	3	-2	4

-5 -4 -3 -2 -1 1 2 3 4 5

MATERIALS

Integer Game Board; counters: 10 each of 2 colors;
2 paper clips

DIRECTIONS

1. Choose the counter color that will mark your plays.
2. If you are Player 1, place the paper clips on any 2 integers at the bottom of the Game Board. Find the sum of your integers, then place one of your counters on a space containing that sum.
3. If you are Player 2, move just one of the paper clips to another integer at the bottom of the Game Board. Find the sum and place a counter on a space containing the sum. **Explain** your move. **(I already have a counter on −7, so I'll move a clip to make a sum of 2. That gives me 2 in a row.)**
4. Take turns moving one clip, finding the sum, and covering the sum with a counter.
5. If you are first to get 4 counters in a row vertically, or horizontally, you win.

If I can get a sum of 2,
I'll have 2 in a row and block you
from getting 4 in the bottom row.
I'll move the clip from 5 to 4.

PROBLEM SOLVING

Name ______________________________

Problem Solving: Adding Integers

DIRECTIONS

- Solve the problem. Circle the strategies you use.
- Show your work and complete the answer.

POSSIBLE STRATEGIES

- Guess, Check, and Revise
- Look for Patterns
- Other: ____________

PROBLEM 1

Use the pattern in the sum of 10 integers to find the sum of the first 100 integers in the same pattern.

A. $1 + (-2) + 3 + (-4) + 5 + (-6) + 7 + (-8) + 9 + (-10) =$ ________

B. $1 + (-2) + 3 + \ldots + 97 + (-98) + 99 + (-100) =$ ________

PROBLEM 2

Use the pattern in the sum of 10 integers to find the sum of the first 100 integers in the same pattern.

A. $2 + (-4) + 6 + (-8) + 10 + (-12) + 14 + (-16) + 18 + (-20) =$ ________

B. $2 + (-4) + 6 + \ldots + (-196) + 198 + (-200) =$ ________

ANALYZE YOUR WORK

What patterns did you find that made it easier to solve the problems?

____

____

____

____

____

PRACTICE TODAY'S NUMBER $-\frac{1}{2}$

Name ______________________

NUMBER AND OPERATIONS

Write the fractions in order from least to greatest. ◂1–3. MOC 049

1. $\frac{5}{4}, \frac{2}{4}, \frac{3}{4}, \frac{7}{4}$ ______________________

2. $\frac{1}{8}, \frac{1}{2}, \frac{3}{8}, \frac{4}{3}$ ______________________

3. $\frac{1}{8}, -\frac{1}{2}, -\frac{3}{8}, -\frac{4}{3}, \frac{1}{2}$ ______________________

Write each product or quotient. ◂4–9. MOC 160–164, 187–193

4. $-\frac{1}{2} \times \frac{1}{4} =$ ________

5. $-\frac{1}{2} \times 4 =$ ________

6. $-\frac{1}{2} \div \frac{1}{2} =$ ________

7. $(-\frac{1}{2})^3 =$ ________

8. $\frac{1}{2} \div (-\frac{1}{4}) =$ ________

9. $(-\frac{1}{2})^4 =$ ________

PATTERNS AND ALGEBRA

Solve for *n*. ◂10–12. MOC 160–164

10. $\frac{1}{2}n = 8; n =$ ________

11. $\frac{1}{2}n = -8; n =$ ________

12. Explain why a rational number like $-\frac{1}{2}$ can be written as $\frac{-1}{2}$, $-(\frac{1}{2})$, or $\frac{1}{-2}$.

____

Fill in the blanks in the pattern and answer the related question. ◂13–14. MOC 193

13. −16, 8, −4, 2, ________, ________

14. How can you tell whether a term will be positive or negative?

____

GEOMETRY AND MEASUREMENT

Draw the polygon and answer the related question. ◀15. MOC 318–320, 351–353 16. MOC 367

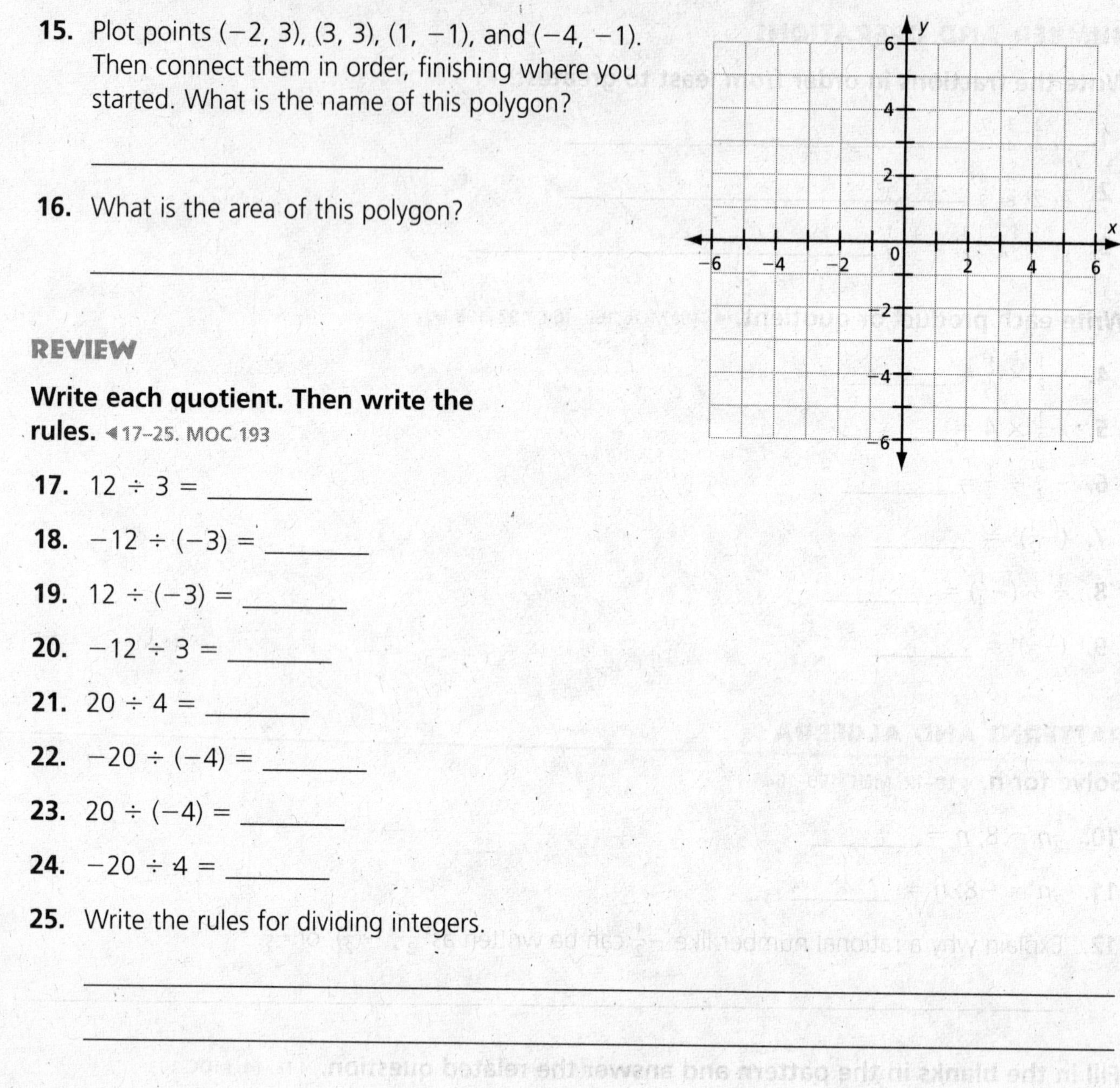

15. Plot points (−2, 3), (3, 3), (1, −1), and (−4, −1). Then connect them in order, finishing where you started. What is the name of this polygon?

____

16. What is the area of this polygon?

____

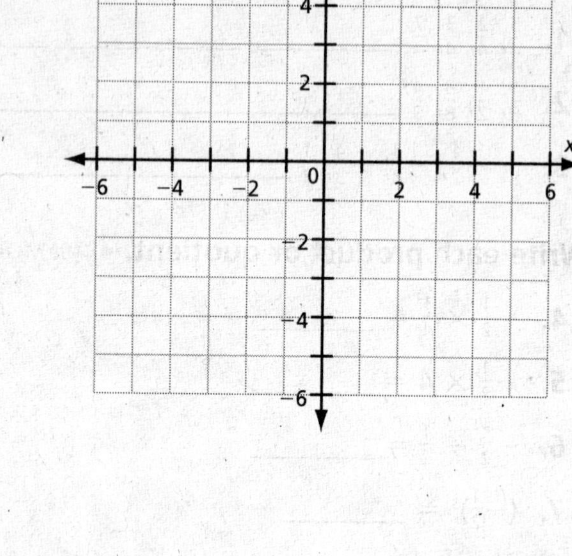

REVIEW

Write each quotient. Then write the rules. ◀17–25. MOC 193

17. $12 \div 3 =$ ________

18. $-12 \div (-3) =$ ________

19. $12 \div (-3) =$ ________

20. $-12 \div 3 =$ ________

21. $20 \div 4 =$ ________

22. $-20 \div (-4) =$ ________

23. $20 \div (-4) =$ ________

24. $-20 \div 4 =$ ________

25. Write the rules for dividing integers.

____

____

GLOSSARY TO GO

Write definitions and draw pictures illustrating new math terms. The vocabulary should be covered in your class time, so you should be familiar with most of the terms.

PROBLEM SOLVING

Name ______________________________

Problem Solving: Integer Magic Squares

DIRECTIONS

- Solve the problem. Circle the strategies you use.
- Show your work and complete the answer on page 72.

POSSIBLE STRATEGIES

- Guess, Check and Revise
- Use Logical Reasoning
- Work Backward
- Write an Equation
- Other: ___________

PROBLEM 1

In a magic square, there is a different number in each box. The sum of the numbers in every row, column and diagonal is the same. The sum in this magic square is 14. Fill in the missing numbers.

PROBLEM 2

The sum in this magic square is −10. Fill in the missing numbers.

ANALYZE YOUR WORK

1. Did your work on the first problem help you with the second problem? If so, how?

____

2. What do you need to know to solve these problems?

____

____

Problem Solving: Integer Magic Squares

1.

−4	3		
7		−2	
	−3	11	
		0	−1

2.

−10		−1	
	2		−5
			−2
3	0		−7

PRACTICE TODAY'S NUMBER $-\frac{1}{4}$

Name ____________________

NUMBER AND OPERATIONS

Write the fractions in order from least to greatest. ◀1–2. MOC 049

1. $\frac{1}{4}, -\frac{3}{4}, \frac{5}{4}, -\frac{1}{4}$ ____________________

2. $\frac{1}{2}, -\frac{1}{2}, \frac{1}{4}, -\frac{1}{4}, \frac{1}{8}, -\frac{1}{8}$ ____________________

Write the value of each expression. ◀3–8. MOC 050, 071, 191, 193

3. $(-\frac{1}{4})^2 =$ ________

4. $(-\frac{1}{4})^3 =$ ________

5. $|-\frac{1}{4}|$ ________

6. $\frac{1}{4} \div \frac{1}{4} =$ ________

7. $-\frac{1}{4} \div \frac{1}{4} =$ ________

8. $(\frac{1}{4})^3 \div (\frac{1}{4})^2 =$ ________

PATTERNS AND ALGEBRA

Solve for *n*. ◀9–10. MOC 107–108, 135–136, 241

9. $n + \frac{3}{4} = \frac{1}{2}$; $n =$ ________

10. $n - (-1\frac{1}{4}) = -1$; $n =$ ________

Continue the pattern and use it for problem 12. ◀11–12. MOC 108

11. $-\frac{3}{4}, -\frac{1}{2}, -\frac{1}{4}, 0,$ ________, ________, ________

12. Describe in general how you would find the next term of this pattern.

____

GEOMETRY AND MEASUREMENT

Draw the polygon and answer the related questions. ◂13. MOC 318–320 14. MOC 349 15–16. MOC 386–389

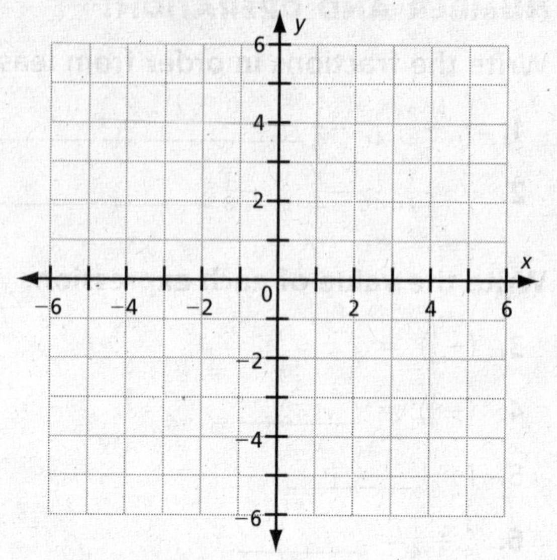

13. Plot points (−1, 2), (1, 2), (0, −1). Then connect them in order, finishing where you started. What is the name of this polygon? Be as specific as possible.

____

14. At what point does the height of the figure intersect the base?

____

15. Name at least 2 special things about the segment from (0, 2) to (0, −1).

____

____

16. How many degrees will the figure rotate before it matches itself exactly? __________

REVIEW

Write the value of each expression. Then answer the related question. ◂17–23. MOC 071

17. $(-\frac{1}{2})^1 =$ ______ **18.** $(-\frac{1}{2})^2 =$ ______

19. $(-\frac{1}{2})^3 =$ ______ **20.** $(-\frac{1}{2})^4 =$ ______

21. $(-\frac{1}{2})^5 =$ ______ **22.** $(-\frac{1}{2})^6 =$ ______

23. What pattern do you see that relates the exponent to the value of the expression?

____

____

GLOSSARY TO GO

Review the definitions and illustrations you added to your Glossary this week. Make additions or corrections if you need to.

Name ______________________________

Problem Solving: Fraction Magic Squares

DIRECTIONS

- Solve the problem. Circle the strategies you use.
- Show your work and complete the answer on page 76.

POSSIBLE STRATEGIES

- Guess, Check and Revise
- Make a Table or an Organized List
- Other: ____________

PROBLEM 1

In this magic square, the sum in every row, column, and diagonal is $2\frac{1}{2}$. Fill in the blank squares using these numbers: $\frac{1}{3}$, $\frac{1}{2}$, $\frac{2}{3}$, $\frac{1}{6}$, $\frac{5}{6}$, $1\frac{1}{2}$, $1\frac{1}{3}$, $1\frac{1}{6}$, 1.

PROBLEM 2

In this magic square, the sum in every row, column, and diagonal is 1. Fill in the blank squares using these numbers: $\frac{1}{2}$, $\frac{1}{6}$, $\frac{1}{3}$, $1\frac{1}{6}$, 1, $1\frac{1}{3}$, $-\frac{1}{2}$, $-\frac{1}{3}$, $-\frac{2}{3}$.

ANALYZE YOUR WORK

1. Did your work on the first problem help you with the second problem? If so, how?

____

2. Which problem was more difficult for you? What made it more difficult? ____________

____

____

____

Problem Solving: Fraction Magic Squares

1.

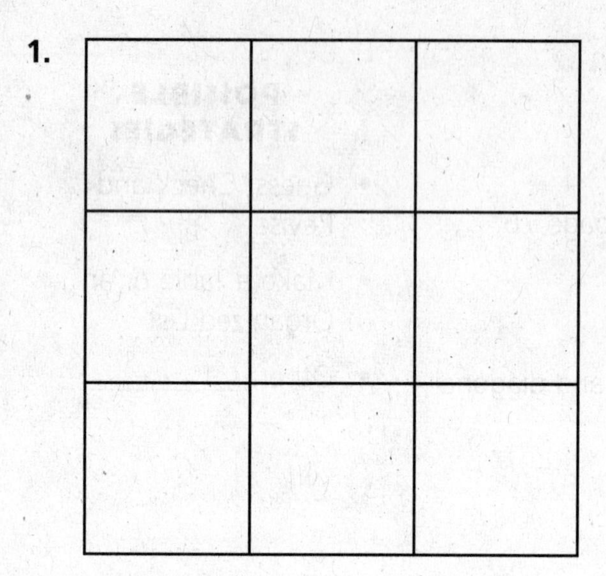

2.

NEWSLETTER

Summer Success: Math

This week, your child has been working with negative numbers. These are found in the real world in winter temperatures, below sea-level elevations, and accounting.

A very good model for positive and negative numbers is a number line.

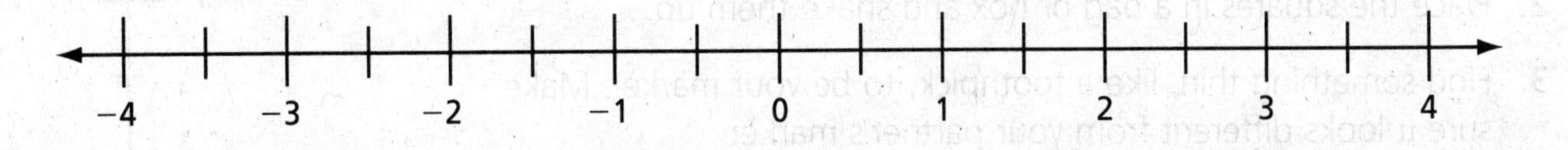

A number line shows that every positive number has an opposite, which is the same distance away from 0, in the opposite direction. So, −1 and 1 are opposites. So are $-2\frac{1}{2}$ and $2\frac{1}{2}$. The only number that you can place on a number line that doesn't have an opposite is 0.

On the back of this page is a game you and your child can play that reinforces ideas about working with positive and negative numbers.

Enjoy your time with your child, and thank you for helping to strengthen your child's comfort with important math concepts.

Number Line Race

MATERIALS

paper, scissors, pencil, small bag or box, toothpicks

DIRECTIONS

1. Cut up 18 small squares of paper. Write one of these numbers on each square:

   $0, 0, \frac{1}{4}, -\frac{1}{4}, \frac{1}{2}, -\frac{1}{2}, \frac{3}{4}, -\frac{3}{4}, 1, -1, 1\frac{1}{2}, -1\frac{1}{2}, 2, -2, 2\frac{1}{2}, -2\frac{1}{2}, 3, -3$

2. Place the squares in a bag or box and shake them up.
3. Find something thin, like a toothpick, to be your marker. Make sure it looks different from your partner's marker.
4. Place your marker and your partner's marker at 0 on the number line.
5. Shake the bag and pick 2 paper squares. Add the numbers and decide whether to move your toothpick that far or to give up your turn. Return your squares to the bag.
6. The first player to land exactly on either end of the number line wins.

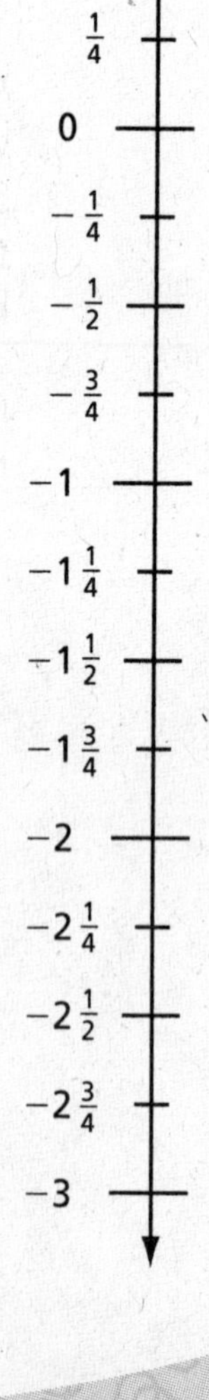

Ask your child for help so he or she can show off this week's successes.

PRACTICE TODAY'S NUMBER $\sqrt{4}$

Name ______________________________

NUMBER AND OPERATIONS

Write the value of the square of each number. ◂1–4. MOC 076

1. −6 __________
2. 11 __________
3. −9 __________
4. −12 __________

Find the values. ◂5–7. MOC 076–077

5. $\sqrt{4}$ __________ and $-\sqrt{4}$ __________
6. $\sqrt{16}$ __________ and $-\sqrt{16}$ __________
7. What does the radical sign ($\sqrt{\ }$) tell you to do?

____

PATTERNS AND ALGEBRA

Continue the pattern and use it for problem 9. 8–9. MOC 076

8. 1, 4, 9, 16, 25, __________, __________, __________,
9. Describe how to find the value of the twelfth term.

____

GEOMETRY AND MEASUREMENT

For each triangle, find the length of the hypotenuse and the area. ◂10–12. MOC 356, 359

10. 6 in. 8 in.

hypotenuse __________

area __________

11. 8 cm 15 cm

hypotenuse __________

area __________

12. 0.3 m 0.4 m

hypotenuse __________

area __________

REVIEW

Write each square or square root. Then use the pattern to help with problem 25. ◀13–25. MOC 076

13. 7^2 = ________

14. 8^2 = ________

15. 9^2 = ________

16. 10^2 = ________

17. 11^2 = ________

18. 12^2 = ________

19. $\sqrt{49}$ = ________

20. $\sqrt{64}$ = ________

21. $\sqrt{81}$ = ________

22. $\sqrt{100}$ = ________

23. $\sqrt{121}$ = ________

24. $\sqrt{144}$ = ________

25. Describe what happens when you square a number and then take the square root of the answer.

____

GLOSSARY TO GO

Write definitions and draw pictures illustrating new math terms. The vocabulary should be covered in your class time, so you should be familiar with most of the terms.

Integer Differences

Object: Find 4 integer differences in a row on the Game Board.

MATERIALS

Integer Game Board; counters, 10 each of 2 colors; 2 paper clips

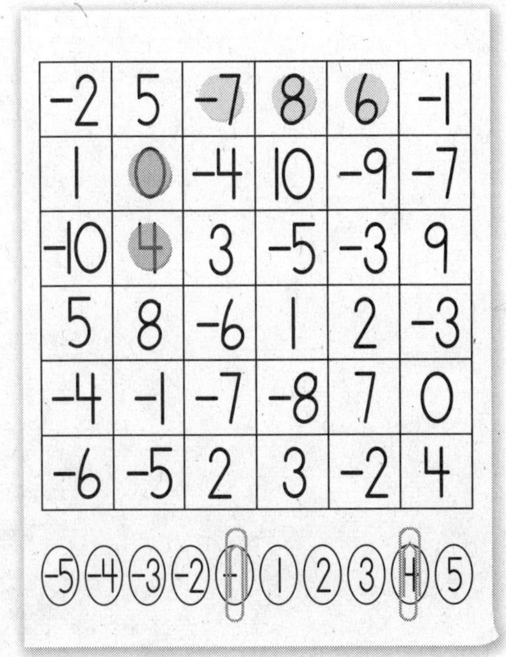

DIRECTIONS

1. Choose the counter color that will mark your plays.
2. If you are Player 1, place the paper clips on any 2 integers at the bottom of the Game Board. Decide how to subtract your integers, then place one of your counters on a space containing that difference.
3. If you are Player 2, move just one of the paper clips to another integer at the bottom of the Game Board. Choose a difference and place a counter on a space containing the difference. **Explain** your decisions. **(I have counters on 4 and 0, so I'd like to find a difference of 5 or 8. If I leave a clip on 4 and move a clip to −1, I can use 4 − (−1) to get 5.)**
4. Take turns moving one clip, finding the difference, and covering the difference with a counter.
5. If you are first to get 4 counters in a row vertically, horizontally, or diagonally, you win.

I have counters on 4 and 0, so I'd like to find a difference of 5 or 8. Five is better because it also blocks you. If I leave a clip on 4 and move a clip to –1, I can use 4 – (–1) to get 5.

Name ______________________

Making a Scatter Plot

Do soccer players who have more assists score more goals?

DIRECTIONS

- Work with a partner.
- Use the blank plot on page 84.
- Decide on scales and intervals for both axes of your plot.
- Title your plot and plot the data for Assists and Goals.
- Answer the questions to analyze the data.

NCAA Division I Women's Soccer 2004–2005 Leading Scorers

Player	Assists	Goals	Games
Debs Brereton	9	19	19
Catherine Burnley	2	15	13
Sonia Curvelo	5	16	16
Aisha Horne	1	23	20
Esmeralda Negron	12	20	22
Candace Nzekor	6	20	20
Emily Parmarter	1	21	18
Katie Thorlakson	24	23	27
Tiffany Weimer	12	26	23
Leeanna Woodworth	15	22	20

Source: NCAA.org

ANALYZE THE DATA

1. What are the ranges in number of assists and goals?

   Assists: ________

   Goals: ________

2. What conclusion can you draw from your scatter plot about whether there is a correlation between goals and assists?

   ____

   ____

Making a Scatter Plot

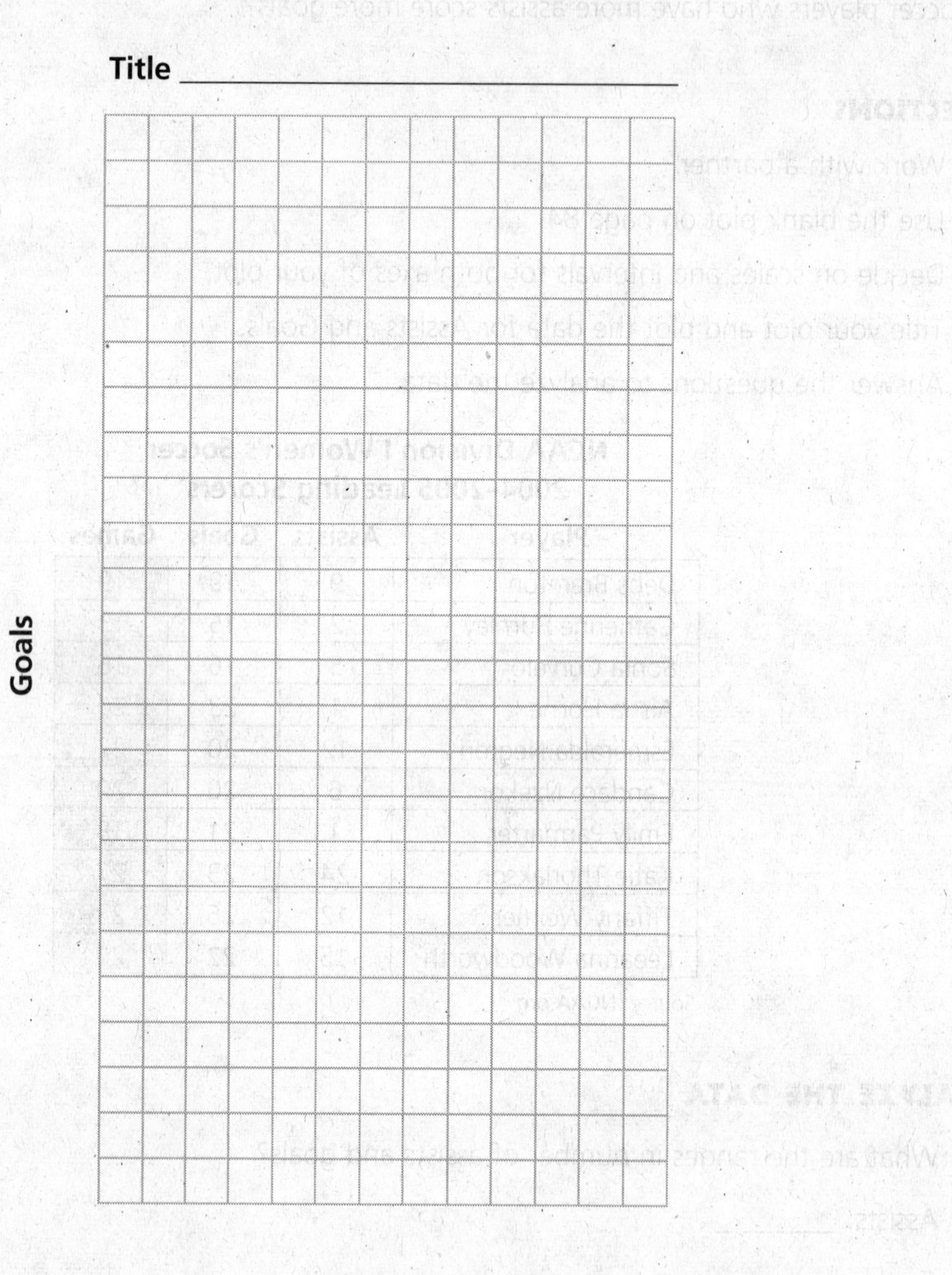

PRACTICE TODAY'S NUMBER $\sqrt{10}$

Name ____________________

NUMBER AND OPERATIONS

Write the square root of each perfect square in this list. Ignore non-perfect squares. ◂1–12. MOC 083

1. 8 ________ **2.** 9 ________

3. 10 ________ **4.** 15 ________

5. 40 ________ **6.** 49 ________

7. 50 ________ **8.** 64 ________

9. 80 ________ **10.** 100 ________

11. 121 ________ **12.** 160 ________

Simplify each expression if you can. You do not need to find roots of non-perfect squares. ◂13–16. MOC 076

13. $\sqrt{3} + \sqrt{3} =$ ________ **14.** $\sqrt{3} + \sqrt{2} =$ ________

15. $\sqrt{2} \times \sqrt{3} =$ ________ **16.** $\sqrt{3} \times \sqrt{12} =$ ________

PATTERNS AND ALGEBRA

Write an equation to help you answer each question. ◂17–19. MOC 366

17. A square has a side-length of $\frac{1}{2}$ foot. What is its area?

____

18. A square has a side length of 0.25 meters. What is its area

____

19. The area of a square is 0.25 square inches. What is the length of a side?

____

GEOMETRY AND MEASUREMENT

Use the diagram to answer the questions. ◂20–24. MOC 376–377

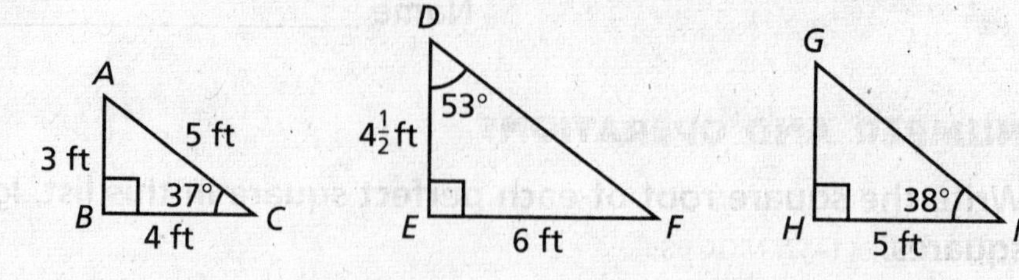

20. Which triangles are similar? ______

21. What is the measure of angle *A*? ______

22. Can you find the length of segment *DF*? If so, what is it? ______

23. Can you find the length of segment *GI*? If so, what is it? ______

24. Explain how you decided on your answer to question 20.

______

______

______

______

REVIEW

Complete the table by writing the square of each given number. Then, answer the questions. ◂25–28. MOC 079

25.

Number	Square
6	
−7	
8	
−9	
10	
−11	
12	
−13	

26. What is the positive square root of 121? ______

27. What is the negative square root of 169? ______

28. Between which 2 whole numbers is the square root of 79?

______

GLOSSARY TO GO

Write definitions and draw pictures illustrating new math terms. The vocabulary should be covered in your class time, so you should be familiar with most of the terms.

Name ______________________

Drawing a Line of Best Fit

About how many goals might a leading soccer player be able to score in 30 games?

DIRECTIONS

- Work with a partner and use the blank plot on page 88.
- Decide on scales and intervals for both axes of your plot.
- Title your plot and plot the data for Games and Goals.
- Find the mean of each set of data and plot that point.
- Sketch a line of best fit. Be sure that it includes the mean.
- Answer the questions to analyze the data.

ANALYZE THE DATA

NCAA Division I Women's Soccer 2004–2005 Leading Scorers

Player	Assists	Goals	Games
Debs Brereton	9	19	19
Catherine Burnley	2	15	13
Sonia Curvelo	5	16	16
Aisha Horne	1	23	20
Esmeralda Negron	12	20	22
Candace Nzekor	6	20	20
Emily Parmarter	1	21	18
Katie Thorlakson	24	23	27
Tiffany Weimer	12	26	23
Leeanna Woodworth	15	22	20

Source: NCAA.org

1. What are the ranges in the number of games played and the number of goals scored?

Games: __________

Goals: __________

2. Look at the line of best fit. Its slope should be about 1. What is the slope telling you about the average number of goals per game by each player?

____

____

3. What conclusions can you draw from your scatter plot and the line of best fit?

____

____

Drawing a Line of Best Fit

Title ______________________________

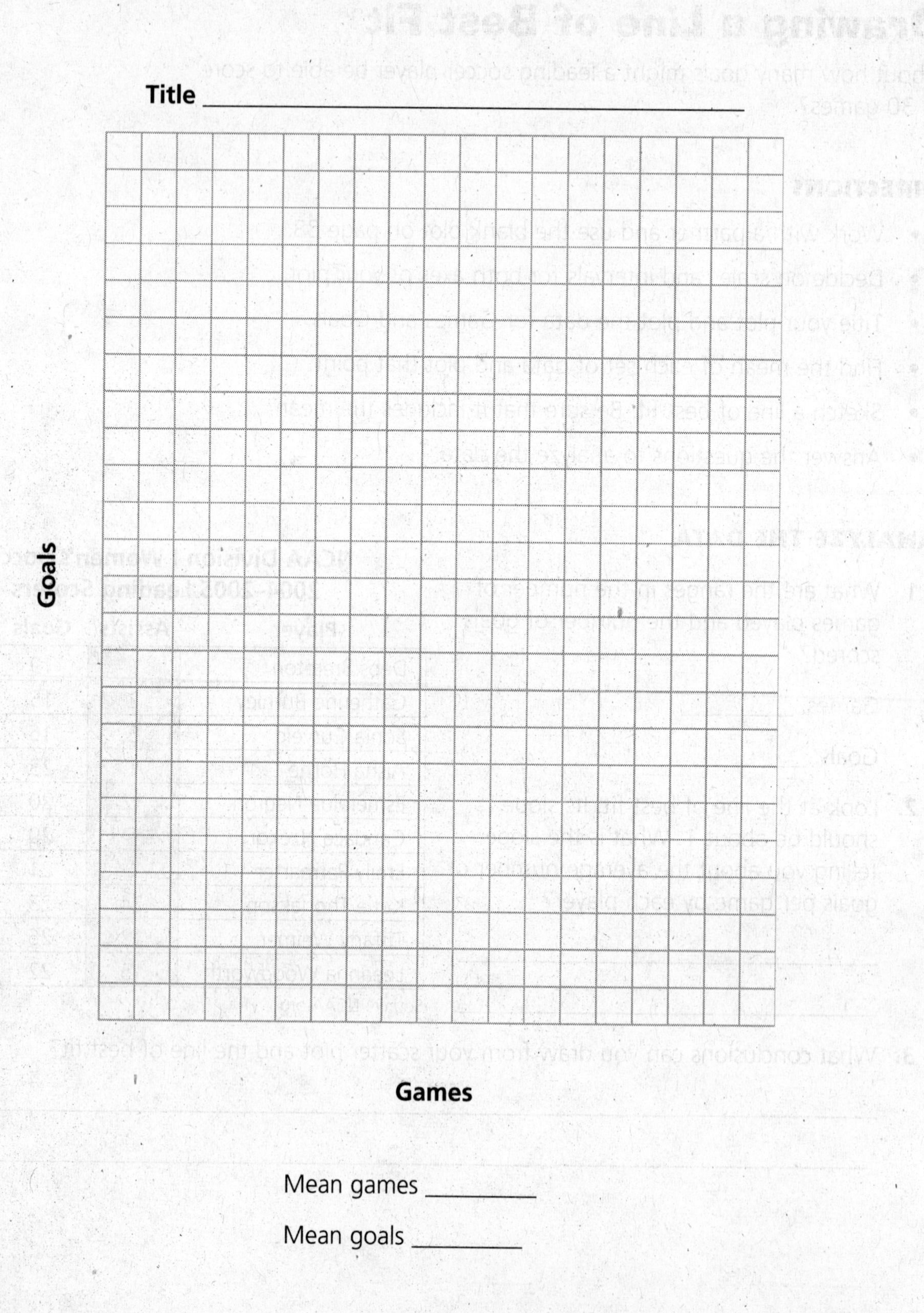

Mean games ________

Mean goals ________

PRACTICE TODAY'S NUMBER 8.64×10^4

Name ____________________

NUMBER AND OPERATIONS

Write each number in standard form and in word form. ◂1–2. MOC 005, 016

1. 5.06×10^5 ____________, ______________________________

2. 1.9×10^6 ____________, ______________________________

Write each number in scientific notation. ◂3–4. MOC 005, 016

3. The area of the Sahara Desert in Africa is about 3,500,000 square miles. ____________

4. The area of the Gobi Desert in China is about 500,000 square miles. ____________

Compute. Write the answer in scientific notation. ◂5. MOC 005, 016

5. The area of Cuba is about 44,200 square miles. The area of Great Britain is about twice the area of Cuba. What is the approximate area of Great Britain? ____________

PATTERNS AND ALGEBRA

Use the Distributive Property to help you write 2 different expressions for each problem. ◂6–7. MOC 204

6. Double one less than the square root of a number ____________

7. Two times the quantity that is 2 more than the square of a number

____

GEOMETRY

Draw the figure then answer the related questions. ◂8–10. MOC 325, 334–337

8. Draw a pair of intersecting lines to form 4 angles so that 2 vertical angles are right angles. What kind of lines did you draw?

____

9. What are the measures of the other 2 angles? ____________

10. Compare vertical angles and adjacent angles. ____________

____

REVIEW

Write the area of each triangle. ◂11–13. MOC 356–357

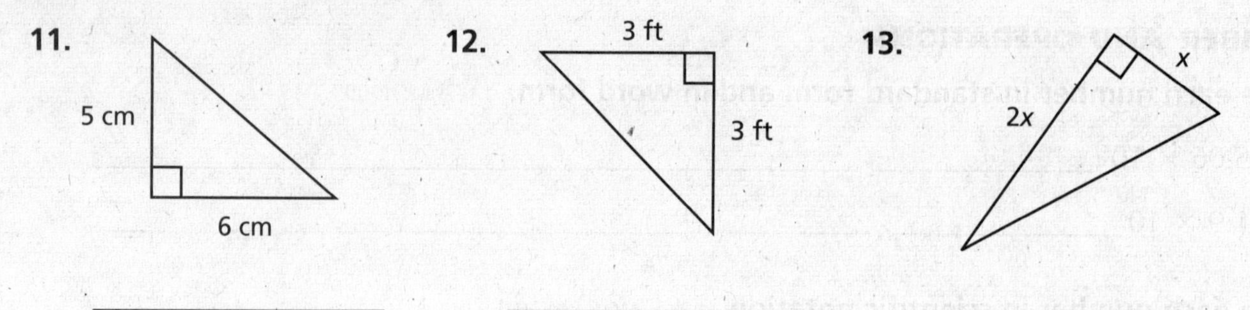

Complete this table. ◂14–15. MOC 006, 015, 071–073

14.

Product of Factors	Product of Powers	Product in Exponential Form	Value
10 × 1	$10^1 \times 10^0$	10^1	
10 × 10			
10 × 100			
100 × 100	$10^2 \times 10^2$	10^4	
10 × 10,000	$10^1 \times 10^4$		
1,000 × 1,000			

15. Look for a pattern in this table and write a rule for multiplying with exponents.

GLOSSARY TO GO

Write definitions and draw pictures illustrating new math terms. The vocabulary should be covered in your class time, so you should be familiar with most of the terms.

GAME

Get to 100

Object: Use percents to create 5 numbers with a sum as close as possible to 100.

MATERIALS

2 sets of 0–9 Digit Cards cardstock, paper, pencils

DIRECTIONS

1. Make your own recording sheet like the one shown. Fill in only the column headings and the percents. Shuffle the Digit Cards and place them in a facedown stack.
2. If you are Player 1, draw 2 cards and use them to make a two-digit number. Choose one of the rows on your recording sheet and place your number in the *Number* column for that row. **Tell why** you chose that row. **(I drew an 8 and a 5. Since there are not many ways to form a larger number, I will use 85 in the 50% row.)** Once a number has been recorded, it cannot be changed. Use mental math to find the given percent of your number and record it in the *Result* column.

3. Return the Digit Cards to the stack, reshuffle, and let Player 2 have a turn.
4. Take turns until both of you have filled in all 5 rows.
5. Add your results. The player closer to 100, either over or under, wins.

There are more ways to get a number less than 85 than a number greater than 85, so I'll put 85 in the 50% row to get the greatest result.

Percent	Number	Result
5%		
10%		
20%		
30%		
50%	85	42.5
	Sum:	

PROBLEM SOLVING

Name ______________________________

Problem Solving: Mystery Integers

DIRECTIONS

- Rewrite the problem in your own words.
- Solve the problem. Circle the strategies you use.
- Show your work and complete the answer.

POSSIBLE STRATEGIES

- Guess, Check, and Revise
- Write an Equation
- Use Logical Reasoning
- Other: ________

PROBLEM 1

Each variable represents a different integer. What does each variable represent in all 4 equations?

$-a \times -a = a$

$b^2 = c$

$b + a = -a$

$c + b - a = a$

$a =$ ________

$b =$ ________

$c =$ ________

PROBLEM 2

Each variable represents a different integer. What does each variable represent in all 4 equations?

$d + 1 = e$

$e + 1 = f$

$d + e = 7$

$d^2 + e^2 = f^2$

$d =$ ________

$e =$ ________

$f =$ ________

ANALYZE YOUR WORK

1. Did your work on the first problem help you with the second problem? If so, how?

____

2. How can you be sure that your solution works? Do you think there could be more than one solution?

____

____

PRACTICE TODAY'S NUMBER 1.0×10^{-3}

Name ______________________________

NUMBER AND OPERATIONS

Write each number as a fraction, a decimal, and in word form. ◂1–3. MOC 014, 044, 073

1. 10^{-4} __________, __________, ____________________
2. 10^{-6} __________, __________, ____________________
3. 10^{-5} __________, __________, ____________________

Write each number in decimal form and in scientific notation. ◂4–6. MOC 016, 044, 073

4. A centimeter is $\frac{1}{100}$ of a meter. __________, __________
5. A milligram is $\frac{1}{1,000}$ of a kilogram. __________, __________
6. When you write out 7.53×10^{-10}, how do you decide how many zeros to write and where to place the decimal point?

____

____

____

____

PATTERNS AND ALGEBRA

Use the diagram to answer the questions. ◂7. MOC 205–209 8. MOC 238–241

7. Each bag contains the same number of apples. There are the same number of apples on each side of the scale. Write an equation to describe this problem.

____

8. How many apples are in each bag? __________ Show your work.

GEOMETRY AND MEASUREMENT

Draw the figure then answer the related questions. ◂9–10. MOC 324, 332–334, 337, 338

9. Draw a pair of parallel lines with a transversal. Number the angles formed. Then, name 4 angles supplementary to your angle 1.

____

____

10. If one of the angles in your drawing is 40°, write and solve equations to find the measures of the other 7 angles.

____

____

____

REVIEW

Write the value of the square of each number. ◂11–13. MOC 076, 083

11. 2 ________ **12.** 3 ________ **13.** 4 ________

Write the positive square root of each number. ◂14–17. MOC 076–077, 083

14. 4 ________ **15.** 9 ________ **16.** 16 ________

17. Compare squaring a number and taking the square root of a number.

____

Write the value of the cube of each number. ◂18–20. MOC 080–083

18. 2 ________ **19.** 3 ________ **20.** 4 ________

GLOSSARY TO GO

Write definitions and draw pictures illustrating new math terms. The vocabulary should be covered in your class time, so you should be familiar with most of the terms.

Name ______________________________

Problem Solving: Rectangular Gardens

DIRECTIONS

- Rewrite the problem in your own words.
- Solve the problem. Circle the strategies you use.
- Show your work. Don't forget the units.

POSSIBLE STRATEGIES

- Guess, Check, and Revise
- Make a Model or a Diagram
- Use Logical Reasoning
- Make a Table or an Organized List
- Other ____________

PROBLEM 1

A. Sally is planning a rectangular garden. She has 14 feet of fence to put around it. If the side lengths are always whole numbers, how many possible rectangles are there?

____

B. The diagonal of the completed garden is 5 feet long. Which size rectangle did Sally use? Explain.

____

____

____

PROBLEM 2

A. List all rectangles with a perimeter of 28 feet that have whole-number dimensions.

____

B. Which of these rectangles has a diagonal 10 feet long?

____

ANALYZE YOUR WORK

What math concepts did you need to know to be able to solve these problems?

____

____

Name ______________________

NUMBER AND OPERATIONS

Answer the questions. ◂ 1. MOC 359 2. MOC 078

1 in.

1. What is the length of the diagonal of this square? ____________

2. Arrange these numbers in order from least to greatest. $\sqrt{4}$, 3, $\sqrt{2}$, 1, $\sqrt{10}$, 4

____

PATTERNS AND ALGEBRA

Solve. ◂3–4. MOC 239

3. The sum of 3 consecutive numbers is 273. Write and solve an equation, then name all 3 numbers.

4. The sum of 3 consecutive even numbers is 606. Write and solve an equation, then name all 3 numbers.

GEOMETRY AND MEASUREMENT

Draw the polygon and answer the related questions. ◂5. MOC 318–320; 6–7. MOC 376–378

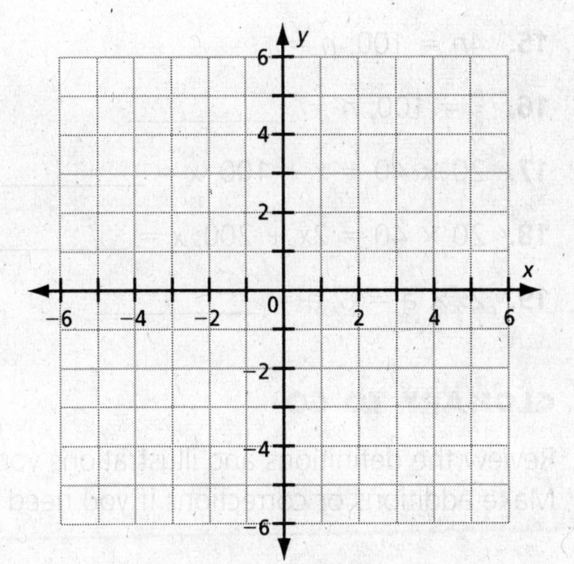

5. Plot a triangle with vertices at points A (−2, 3), B (−2, 0), C (3, 0). Then plot and label the points for figure DEF with legs twice as long and point E at (−6, −2).

6. How does triangle DEF compare to triangle ABC?

____

____

____

7. How does the area of triangle DEF compare to the area of triangle ABC?

____

Draw a diagram of the problem and then solve it. ◀8. MOC 359

8. A tower is 200 feet high. A wire connects the top of the tower to a point on the ground that is 150 feet from the base of the tower. How long is the wire?

____

REVIEW

Write an algebraic expression for each phrase. ◀9–12. MOC 204

9. 6 more than n ___________

10. 5 less than n ___________

11. 3 times n ___________

12. half of n ___________

Solve each problem. ◀13–19. MOC 087, 145, 241–242

13. $n + 10 = 45$; $n =$ ___________

14. $n - 100 = 50$; $n =$ ___________

15. $4n = 100$; $n =$ ___________

16. $\frac{n}{2} = 100$; $n =$ ___________

17. $20 \times 40 = x + 100$; $x =$ ___________

18. $20 \times 40 = 2x + 200$; $x =$ ___________

19. $2^2 \times a = 8$; $a =$ ___________

GLOSSARY TO GO

Review the definitions and illustrations you added to your Glossary this week. Make additions or corrections if you need to.

Name ______________________________

Problem Solving: More Mystery Integers

DIRECTIONS

- Solve the problem. Circle the strategies you use.
- Show your work and complete the answer.

POSSIBLE STRATEGIES

- Guess, Check, and Revise
- Write an Equation
- Use Logical Reasoning
- Other: ____________

PROBLEM 1

Each variable represents a different integer. What does each variable represent in all 4 equations?

$a \times a = b$ $a =$ ________

$a \times b = a$ $b =$ ________

$a - b = c$ $c =$ ________

$2 \times c = -4$

PROBLEM 2

Each variable represents a different one-digit integer. What does each variable represent in all 4 equations?

$d + e = f$ $d =$ ________

$\sqrt{f} = d$ $e =$ ________

$2 \times d = e$ $f =$ ________

$2 \times e = d + f$

ANALYZE YOUR WORK

1. Did your work on the first problem help you with the second problem? If so, how?

____

2. How can you be sure that your solution works? Do you think there could be more than one solution?

____

____

NEWSLETTER

Summer Success: Math

This week, students have been studying powers and roots and their applications. This means they've looked at perfect squares like 4, 9, and 25 and their positive and negative square roots, 2 and −2, 3 and −3, 5 and −5.

We also worked on measurement of length: very great and very small measures and measures you can figure out just by knowing other measures. Ask your child to explain statements like these:

- There are 9.0×10^9 stars in the galaxy. (That's scientific notation for 9 billion.)
- A milliliter is a thousandth of a liter. (There are 1,000 milliliters in a liter.)

On the back of this page is a puzzle that uses powers and roots. Ask your child to show you how to solve it.

Enjoy your time with your child, and thank you for helping to strengthen your child's comfort with important math concepts.

Multiplying Exponential Expressions

Use 3, 4, or 5 digits in a row or column to write equations with powers and roots. For example, | 3 | 6 | 6 | could be used to write $\sqrt{36} = 6$.

4	9	7	8	3
0	6	4	1	6
0	8	1	9	6
2	5	5	6	4
0	1	6	4	8

Enjoy these activities with your child. Remember that using math in the real world will help your child understand that studying math is important in school.

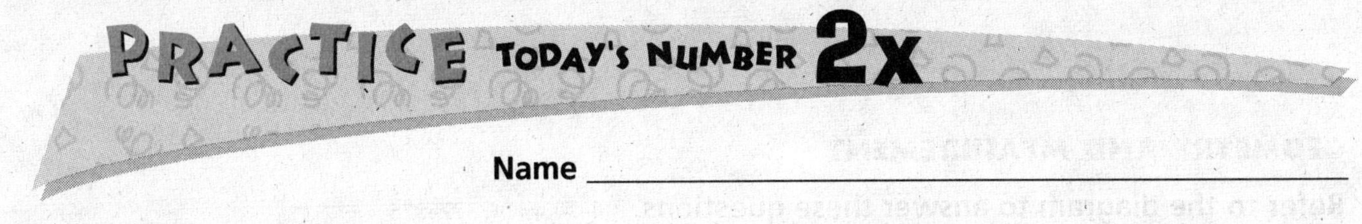

Name ______________________________

NUMBER AND OPERATIONS

Complete each table of values. Graph and label each function on the coordinate grid, and find its slope. ◂1–2. MOC 243, 245–248

1. $y = 2x$; slope ________

x	y
−3	
−2	
−1	
0	
1	
2	

2. $y = 1.5x$; slope ________

x	y
−4	
−2	
0	
1	
2	
3	

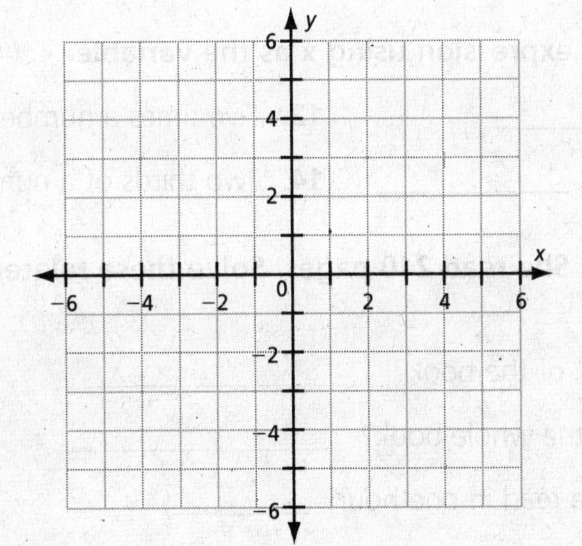

PATTERNS AND ALGEBRA

Analyze the patterns. ◂3–5. MOC 204

3. x, $2x$, $4x$, $8x$, ________, ________, ________

4. x, $3x$, $9x$, $27x$, ________, ________, ________

5. Let x be the term-number. Write algebraic expressions to describe these numerical patterns: 5, 10, 15, 20, . . . and 3, 6, 9, 12, . . .

____

GEOMETRY AND MEASUREMENT

Refer to the diagram to answer these questions. ◀6–10. MOC 372–375

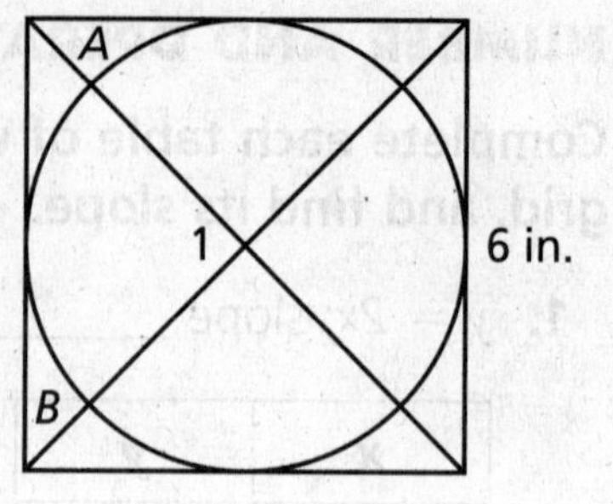

6. The circle is in a square. What is its diameter? ____________

7. What is the circumference of the circle? Leave your answer in terms of π. ____________

8. What is the area of the circle in terms of π? ____________

9. What is the measure of angle 1? Tell how you know.

____

____

____

10. What is the measure of arc *AB*? Tell how you know.

____

REVIEW

For each phrase, write an algebraic expression using x as the variable. ◀11–14. MOC 204

11. Ten less than a number ____________

12. Five times a number ____________

13. One more than 4 times a number ____________

14. Two thirds of a number ____________

Rita read $\frac{2}{3}$ of her book in 10 hours. She read 240 pages. Solve these related problems. ◀15–19. MOC 203–206, 241–242

15. How long did it take her to read $\frac{1}{3}$ of the book? ____________

16. How long will it take her to read the whole book? ____________

17. What fraction of the book did Rita read in one hour? ____________

18. How many pages are in the whole book? ____________

19. How many pages did Rita read in one hour? ____________

GLOSSARY TO GO

Write definitions and draw pictures illustrating new math terms. The vocabulary should be covered in your class time, so you should be familiar with most of the terms.

GAME

Equation Decisions

Object: Write and solve equations. The running sum of the values of *x* must be less than, and as close as possible to, 100.

MATERIALS

Two 1–6 number cubes, 2 sets of 0–9 Digit Cards with the zeros removed

DIRECTIONS

1. If you are Player 2, turn to page 106 and share the recording sheets. Shuffle and stack the Digit Cards in a facedown stack.
2. If you are Player 1, roll the number cubes and pick 2 Digit Cards. Use the faceup numbers on the cubes to make a fraction. Its value can be 1, or greater or less than 1. Write the fraction to the left of *x* on your recording sheet. Use the Digit Cards to make a 2-digit number. Write this number to the right of the equals sign. **Explain why** you used these numbers in your equation. **(If I use 42 and $\frac{2}{3}$, I'll go over 100. If I use 42 and $\frac{3}{2}$, I'll get too close to 100. So, I'll solve $\frac{3}{2}x = 24$.)**
3. Try to use mental math to find the value of *x*. Round to the nearest tenth.
4. Do not return the cards to the deck after you use them. Take turns until you have both solved 4 equations. After 4 rounds, if your running sum is closer to, but still less than, 100, you win.

If I use 42 and $\frac{2}{3}$, I'll go over 100. If I use 42 and $\frac{3}{2}$, I'll get too close to 100. So, I'll solve $\frac{3}{2}x = 24$.

2 4

3 6 5 2 1 4

Round	Equation	Value of *x*	Running Sum
1	$\frac{1}{2}x = 25$	$x = 50$	50
2	$\frac{3}{2}x = 24$	$x = 16$	66
3	___ $x =$ ___	$x =$ ___	
4	___ $x =$ ___	$x =$ ___	

Equation Decisions Recording Sheet

Player 1 ______________________

Round	Equation	Value of x	Running Sum
1	___ x = ___	x = ___	
2	___ x = ___	x = ___	
3	___ x = ___	x = ___	
4	___ x = ___	x = ___	

Round	Equation	Value of x	Running Sum
1	___ x = ___	x = ___	
2	___ x = ___	x = ___	
3	___ x = ___	x = ___	
4	___ x = ___	x = ___	

Round	Equation	Value of x	Running Sum
1	___ x = ___	x = ___	
2	___ x = ___	x = ___	
3	___ x = ___	x = ___	
4	___ x = ___	x = ___	

Round	Equation	Value of x	Running Sum
1	___ x = ___	x = ___	
2	___ x = ___	x = ___	
3	___ x = ___	x = ___	
4	___ x = ___	x = ___	

Player 2 ______________________

Round	Equation	Value of x	Running Sum
1	___ x = ___	x = ___	
2	___ x = ___	x = ___	
3	___ x = ___	x = ___	
4	___ x = ___	x = ___	

Round	Equation	Value of x	Running Sum
1	___ x = ___	x = ___	
2	___ x = ___	x = ___	
3	___ x = ___	x = ___	
4	___ x = ___	x = ___	

Round	Equation	Value of x	Running Sum
1	___ x = ___	x = ___	
2	___ x = ___	x = ___	
3	___ x = ___	x = ___	
4	___ x = ___	x = ___	

Round	Equation	Value of x	Running Sum
1	___ x = ___	x = ___	
2	___ x = ___	x = ___	
3	___ x = ___	x = ___	
4	___ x = ___	x = ___	

Name ______________________________

Looking for Correlations

Are students' ages related to their performance on fitness tests?

DIRECTIONS

- Work with a partner.
- Use the blank scatter plots on page 108.
- Plot the data for *Age* and *Shuttle Run* scores on one plot. Plot *Age* and *Sit and Reach* scores on the other.
- Answer the questions to analyze the data.

School Fitness Test: Mean Scores by Age

Age	Shuttle Run (in sec)	Sit and Reach (in cm)	Sit-Ups	Flexed Arm Hang (in sec)
10	11.8	27	32	10
11	11.4	25	34	9
12	10.9	28	37	10
13	10.5	24	39	11
14	10.2	26	42	13

Source: National Physical Fitness Award results

ANALYZE THE DATA

1. Are you able to sketch a line of best fit for the scatter plot of *Age* and *Shuttle Run* results? What does this tell you about the data?

____

____

2. Are you able to sketch a line of best fit for the scatter plot of *Age* and *Sit and Reach* results? What does this tell you about the data?

____

____

3. Tell whether any correlations you found are positive or negative. Explain how you know.

____

____

Looking for Correlations

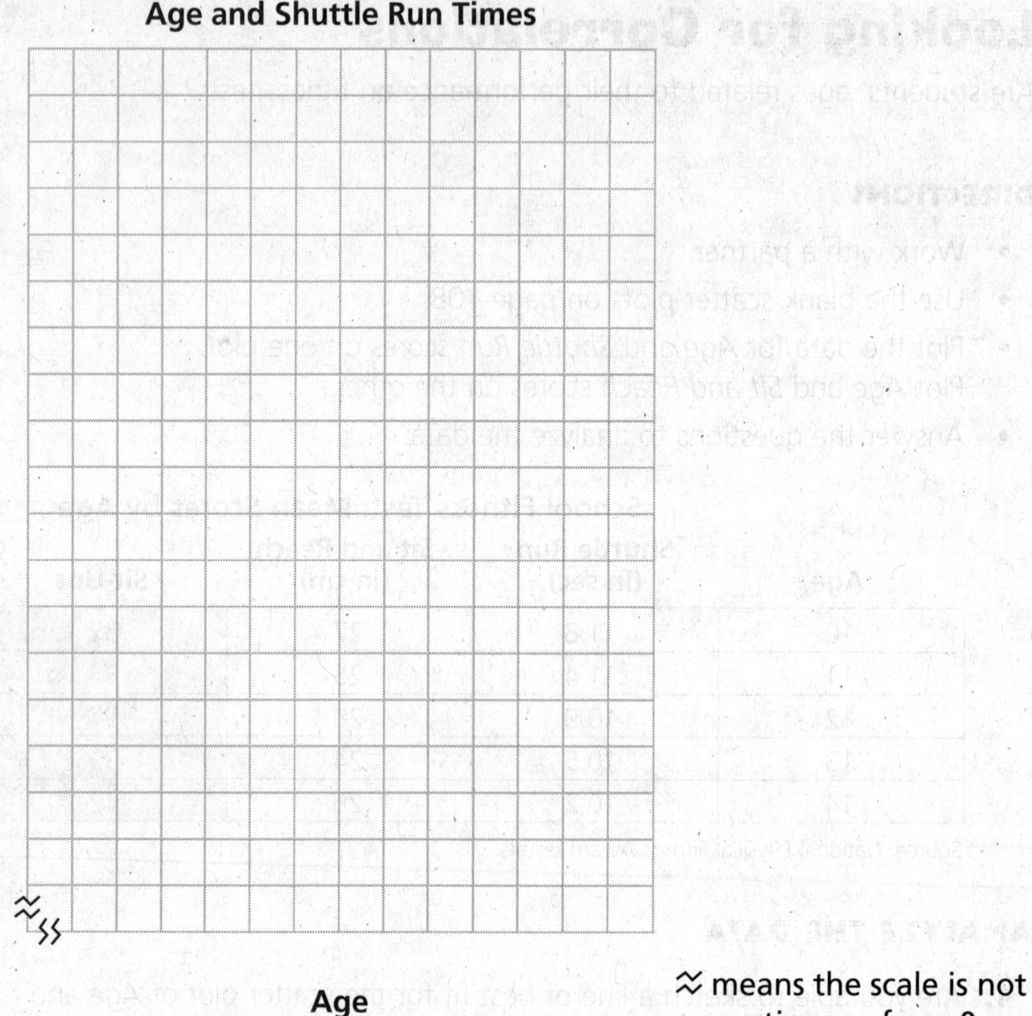

≈ means the scale is not continuous from 0.

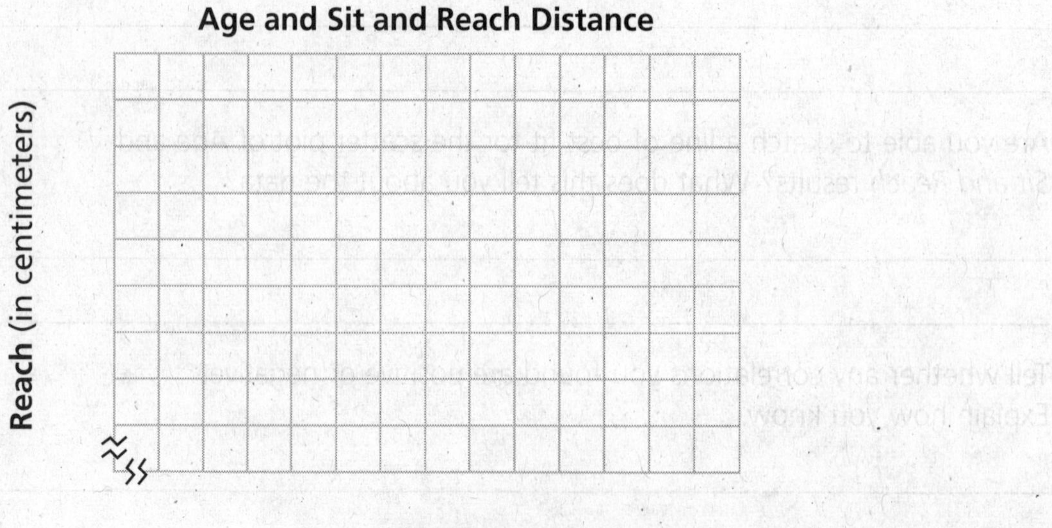

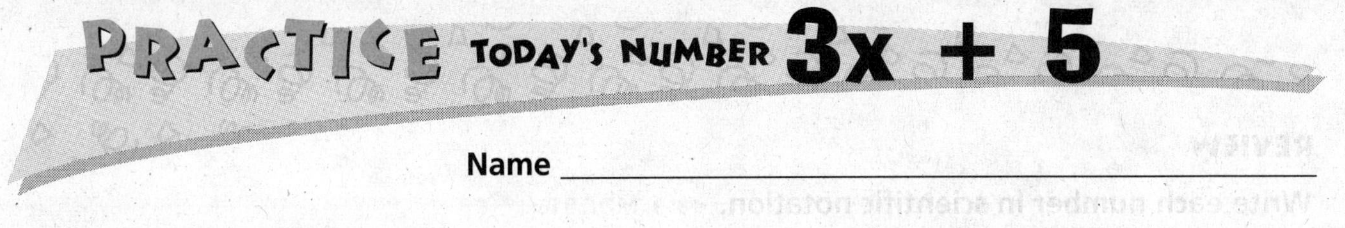

Name ______________________________

NUMBER AND OPERATIONS

Complete each table of values. Then graph and label each function on the coordinate grid. ◀1–2. MOC 243, 245–247

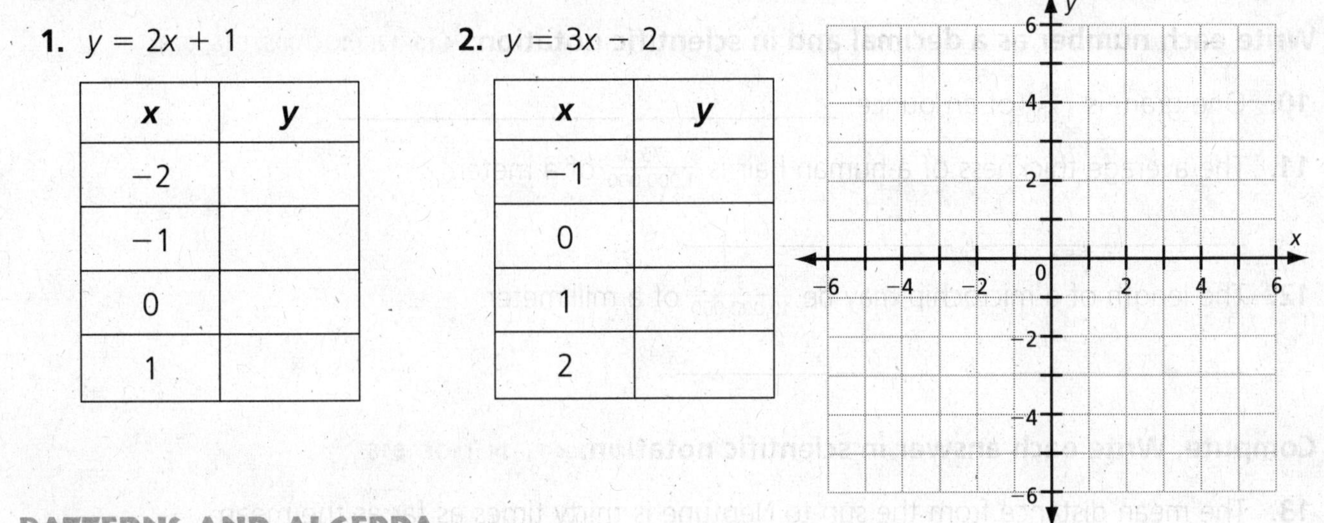

1. $y = 2x + 1$

x	y
−2	
−1	
0	
1	

2. $y = 3x - 2$

x	y
−1	
0	
1	
2	

PATTERNS AND ALGEBRA

Refer to the graphs for questions 1 and 2 to answer these questions. ◀3–5. MOC 245–248

3. What is the slope of $y = 2x + 1$? __________

4. Which graph has a steeper slope? ____________________

5. At what point will the graphs intersect? ____________________

GEOMETRY AND MEASUREMENT

Use the diagram to answer the questions. ◀6–7. MOC 401

6. What is the name of the figure?

____

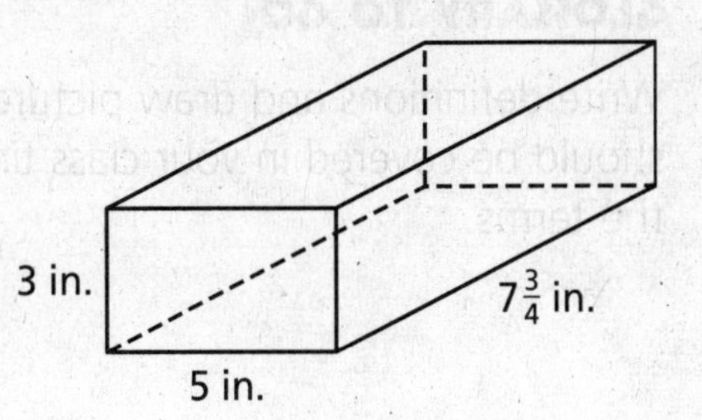

7. What is the surface area of the figure? Show your work.

____

REVIEW

Write each number in scientific notation. ◀8–9. MOC 016

8. The mean distance from the sun to Earth is about 93 million miles. ________________

9. Light can travel about 5,870,000,000,000 miles in one year. ________________

Write each number as a decimal and in scientific notation. ◀10–12. MOC 005, 016, 073

10. One gram is $\frac{35}{1,000}$ of an ounce. ____________, ____________

11. The average thickness of a human hair is $\frac{75}{1,000,000}$ of a meter.

____________, ____________

12. The length of a microchip may be $\frac{3}{10,000,000}$ of a millimeter.

____________, ____________

Compute. Write each answer in scientific notation. ◀13–14. MOC 016

13. The mean distance from the sun to Neptune is thirty times as far as the mean distance of 93 million miles from the sun to Earth. What is the mean distance from the sun to Neptune?

____

14. How much would one million specks of dust weigh if one speck weighs 0.000000000753 kg?

____

GLOSSARY TO GO

Write definitions and draw pictures illustrating new math terms. The vocabulary should be covered in your class time, so you should be familiar with most of the terms.

Name ______________________________

Classifying Correlations: Strong or Weak?

How strong are correlations between students' ages and their fitness?

MATERIALS

Rulers

DIRECTIONS

- Work with a partner. Use the blank scatter plots on page 112.
- Plot the data for *Age* and *Sit-Ups* scores on one plot, and *Age* and *Flexed Arm Hang* scores on the other.
- Answer the questions to analyze the data.

School Fitness Test: Mean Scores by Age

Age	Shuttle Run (in sec)	Sit and Reach (in cm)	Sit-Ups	Flexed Arm Hang (in sec)
10	11.8	27	32	10
11	11.4	25	34	9
12	10.9	28	37	10
13	10.5	24	39	11
14	10.2	26	42	13

Source: National Physical Fitness Award results

ANALYZE THE DATA

1. Can you sketch a line of best fit for each of the scatter plots? What does this tell you about the data?

____

2. Tell whether any correlations you found are positive or negative.

____

3. How closely does your line of best fit match the data? What does this tell you about how strong or weak each correlation is?

____

____

____

Classifying Correlations: Strong or Weak?

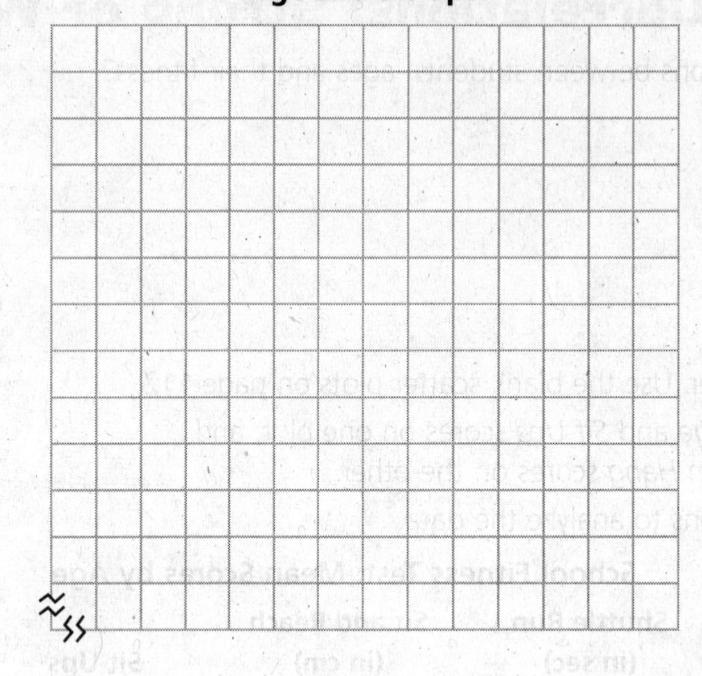

≈ means the scale is not continuous from 0.

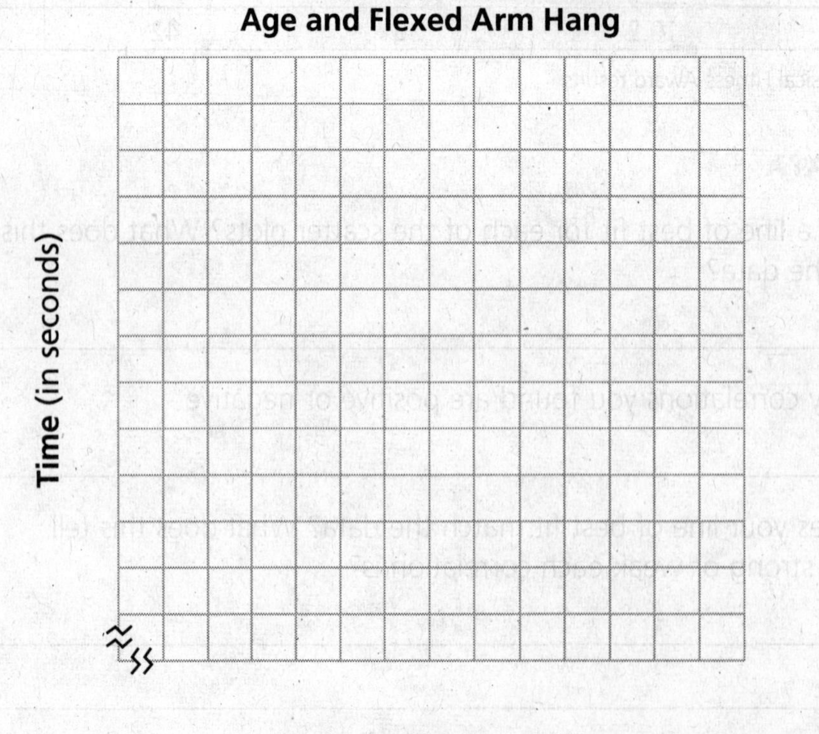

PRACTICE TODAY'S NUMBER $-5x$

Name ______________________________

NUMBER AND OPERATIONS

Complete each table of values. Then answer the related question. ◂1–3. MOC 243, 248–250

1. $y = -3x$

x	y
−3	
−2	
−1	
1	
2	
3	

2. $y = 2.5x$

x	y
−3	
−2	
−1	
1	
2	
3	

3. Both of these functions graph as straight lines. What are their slopes?

$y = -3x$ __________

$y = 2.5x$ __________

PATTERNS AND ALGEBRA

Answer each question. ◂4–6. MOC 248–250

4. Does the table of values in problem 1 describe a line with a positive or negative slope?

____

5. Does the table of values in problem 2 describe a line with a positive or negative slope?

____

6. Explain how you can tell whether the graph of the equation for a line will have a positive or negative slope just by looking at the equation.

____

____

GEOMETRY AND MEASUREMENT

Find the exact surface area of each figure. Show your work. ◂7. MOC 412, 8. MOC 407

7. cylinder: ______________

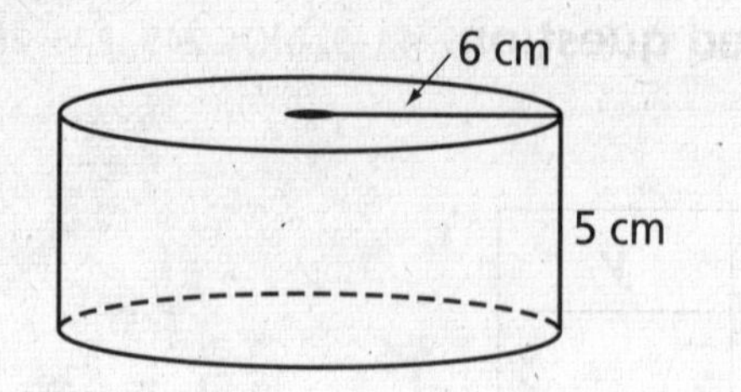

8. pyramid: ______________

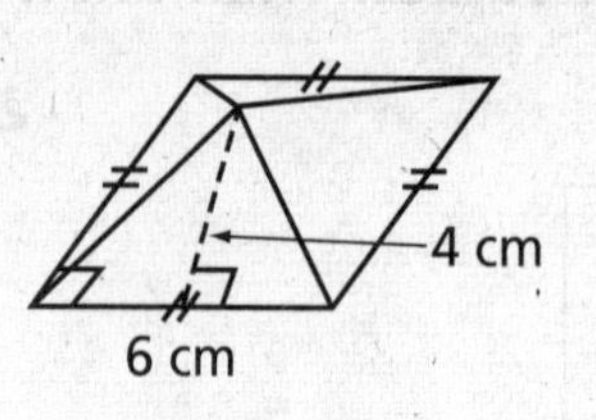

REVIEW

Try to use mental math to solve these related problems. If you need to use pencil and paper, try to do some of the steps using mental math. ◂9–14. MOC 148

9. If a postage stamp costs 37¢, how much will 4 stamps cost? ______________

10. 5 stamps? ______________

11. 8 stamps? ______________

12. 11 stamps? ______________

13. 15 stamps? ______________

14. It costs $3.40 to mail one package. How much will it cost to mail 3 identical packages? ______________

Solve these problems by using proportions. ◂15–17. MOC 428–429

15. It takes you 4 hours to hike 6 miles. At that rate, how many hours does it take you to hike a mile? ______________

16. It takes you 4 hours to hike 6 miles. At that rate, how far can you hike in one hour? ______________

17. To make a punch you mix 2 parts of fruit juice to 3 parts of soda water. How much soda water must you add to 10 cups of fruit juice?

____

GLOSSARY TO GO

Write definitions and draw pictures illustrating new math terms. The vocabulary should be covered in your class time, so you should be familiar with most of the terms.

GAME

Integer Draw

Object: Add and subtract integers to get a number as close as possible to zero.

MATERIALS

Two sets of Integer Cards, paper, pencils

DIRECTIONS

1. Make your own recording sheet like the one shown. Fill in only the column headings and the *Round* column. Shuffle the Integer Cards and place them in a facedown pile.
2. If you are Player 1, draw 3 cards from the pile. Use them to make an expression with one addition and one subtraction operation. The value must be as close as possible to 0. **Tell why** you used that expression. **(I have 2, 4, and −3. If I add 4 and −3, I'll get 1. Then I can subtract 2 to get −1. I could find other expressions with values of 1 and −1, but I can't find any way to get closer to 0.)**
3. Keep track of the value of each expression.
4. Take turns. After 4 rounds, add the integers in the *Value* column. If your sum is closer to 0, you win.

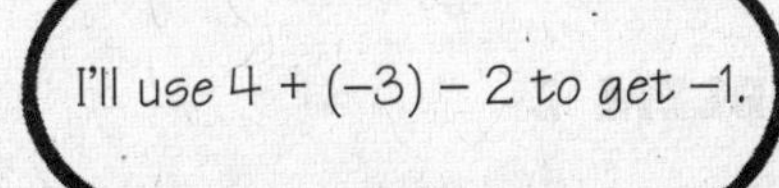

Round	Expression	Value
1	4 + (−3) − 2	−1
2		
3		

Name ______________________________

Problem Solving: Bags of Apples and Pears

POSSIBLE STRATEGIES

- Guess, Check, and Revise
- Write an Equation
- Other: ____________

DIRECTIONS

- Solve the problem and circle the strategies you used.
- Show your work and complete the answer. You may need to use a separate piece of paper.

PROBLEM 1

Each bag on the balance contains the same number of apples. The number of identical apples is the same on both sides of the scale. How many apples are in each bag?

There are _________ apples in each bag.

PROBLEM 2

Each bag on the balance contains the same number of pears. The number of identical pears is the same on both sides of the scale. How many pears are in each bag?

There are _________ pears in each bag.

ANALYZE YOUR WORK

If you did not use the *Write an Equation* strategy, try to write one now for Problem 2.

____

PRACTICE TODAY'S NUMBER $x^2 + 2x$

Name ______________________________

NUMBER AND OPERATIONS

Complete each table of values. Graph and label each function on the coordinate grid. ◂1–3. MOC 243, 251–252

1. $y = x^2 + 3x$

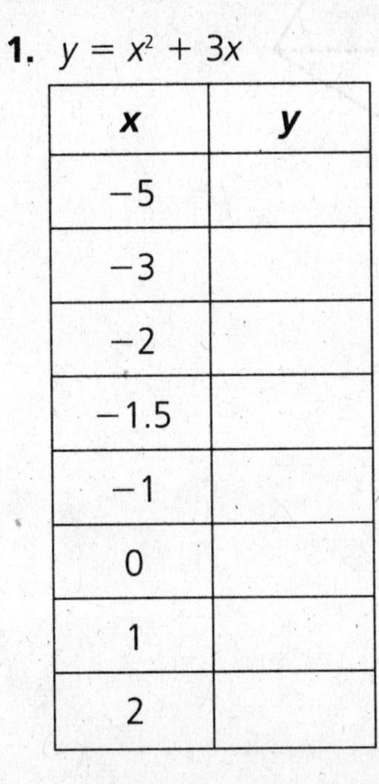

x	y
−5	
−3	
−2	
−1.5	
−1	
0	
1	
2	

2. $y = x^2 - x$

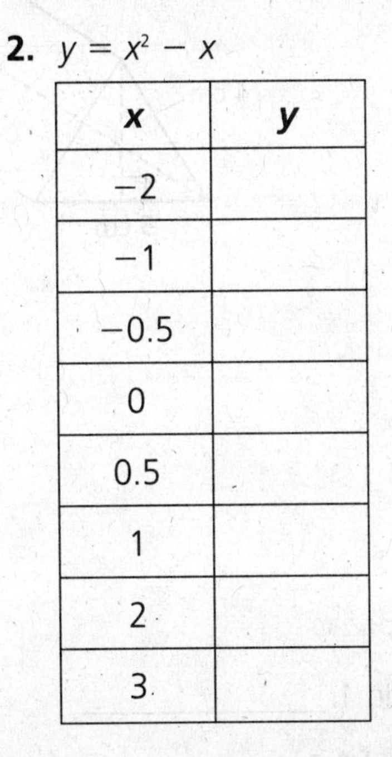

x	y
−2	
−1	
−0.5	
0	
0.5	
1	
2	
3	

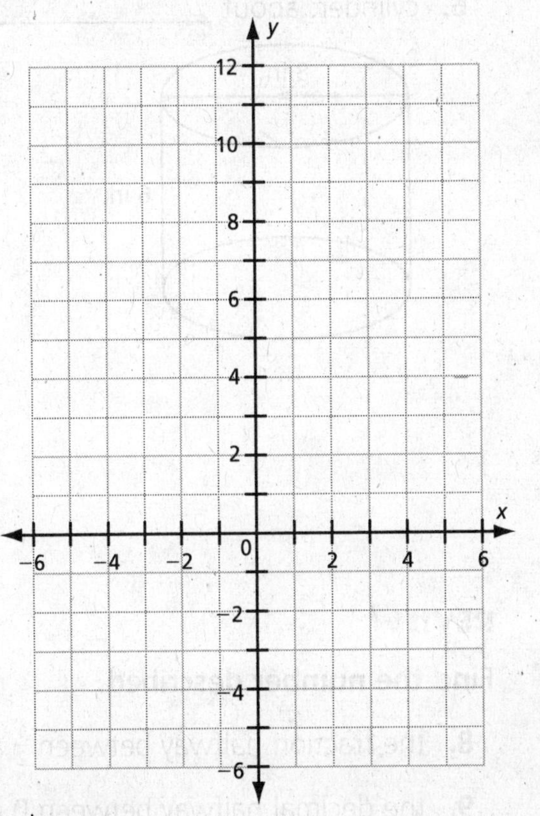

3. Look at your graphs for problems 1 and 2. Describe the shape of the graph of an equation that contains the square of a variable.

____

PATTERNS AND ALGEBRA

Use the diagram to answer questions. ◂4–5. MOC 203–206

4. The length of this rectangle is 2 units greater than its width. Write an expression for the area.

x

____

5. Let y represent the area of the rectangle. Write an equation to find the value of y.

____

GEOMETRY AND MEASUREMENT

Find the volume of each figure. Show your work. Use 3.14 for π. ◀6. MOC 413 7. MOC 397

6. cylinder: about ____________

7. prism: ____________

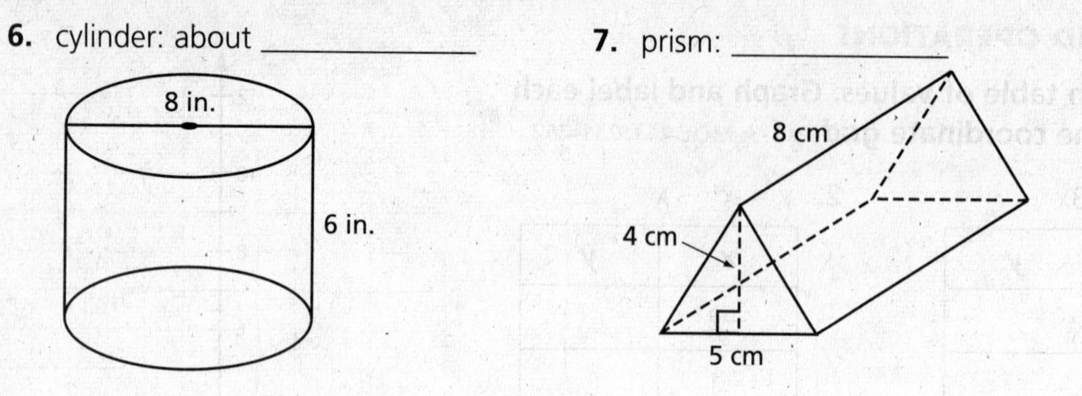

REVIEW

Find the number described. ◀8–14. MOC 230

8. the fraction halfway between $\frac{1}{2}$ and 1 ____________

9. the decimal halfway between 0 and 0.5 ____________

10. the fraction halfway between $\frac{1}{2}$ and $\frac{1}{4}$ ____________

11. the decimal halfway between 0.1 and 0.2 ____________

12. the fraction twice $\frac{1}{6}$ ____________

13. the decimal 0.02 less than 0.6 ____________

14. the fraction $\frac{1}{3}$ more than $\frac{1}{2}$ ____________

GLOSSARY TO GO

Write definitions and draw pictures illustrating new math terms. The vocabulary should be covered in your class time, so you should be familiar with most of the terms.

PROBLEM SOLVING

Name ____________________

Problem Solving: Apples and Tangelos

DIRECTIONS

- Solve the problems and circle the strategies you used.
- Show your work.
- Assume that all apples have the same weight and that all tangelos have the same weight.

POSSIBLE STRATEGIES

- Guess, Check, and Revise
- Write an Equation
- Other: ____________

PROBLEM 1

A. How many tangelos weigh the same as one apple?

____

B. How many apples weigh the same as one tangelo?

____

PROBLEM 2

A. How many tangelos weigh the same as one apple?

____

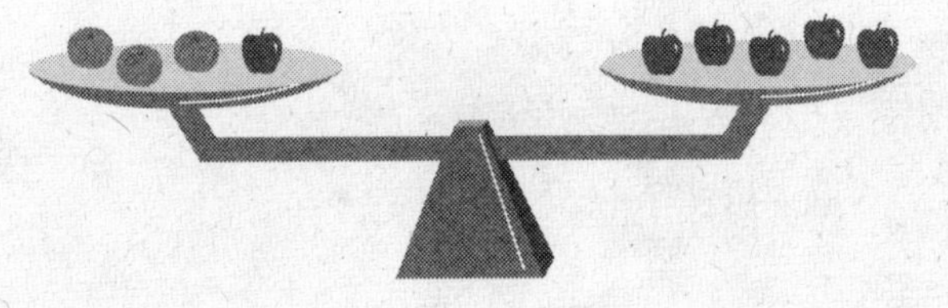

B. How many apples weigh the same as one tangelo?

____

ANALYZE YOUR WORK

As you worked through the problems, how did you make sure that the 2 sides of the equation stayed balanced?

____

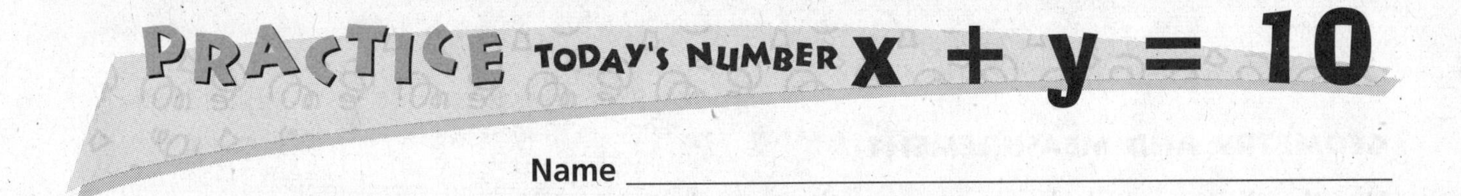

PRACTICE TODAY'S NUMBER $x + y = 10$

Name ____________________

NUMBER AND OPERATIONS

Write 3 possible expressions that fit each description. Try to use positive and negative numbers, fractions, and decimals in your expressions. ◂1–2. MOC 243

1. The sum of 2 numbers is 10. ____________________

2. The difference between 2 numbers is 8. ____________________

PATTERNS AND ALGEBRA

Complete each table of values. Graph and label each function on the coordinate grid. ◂3–4. MOC 243, 247

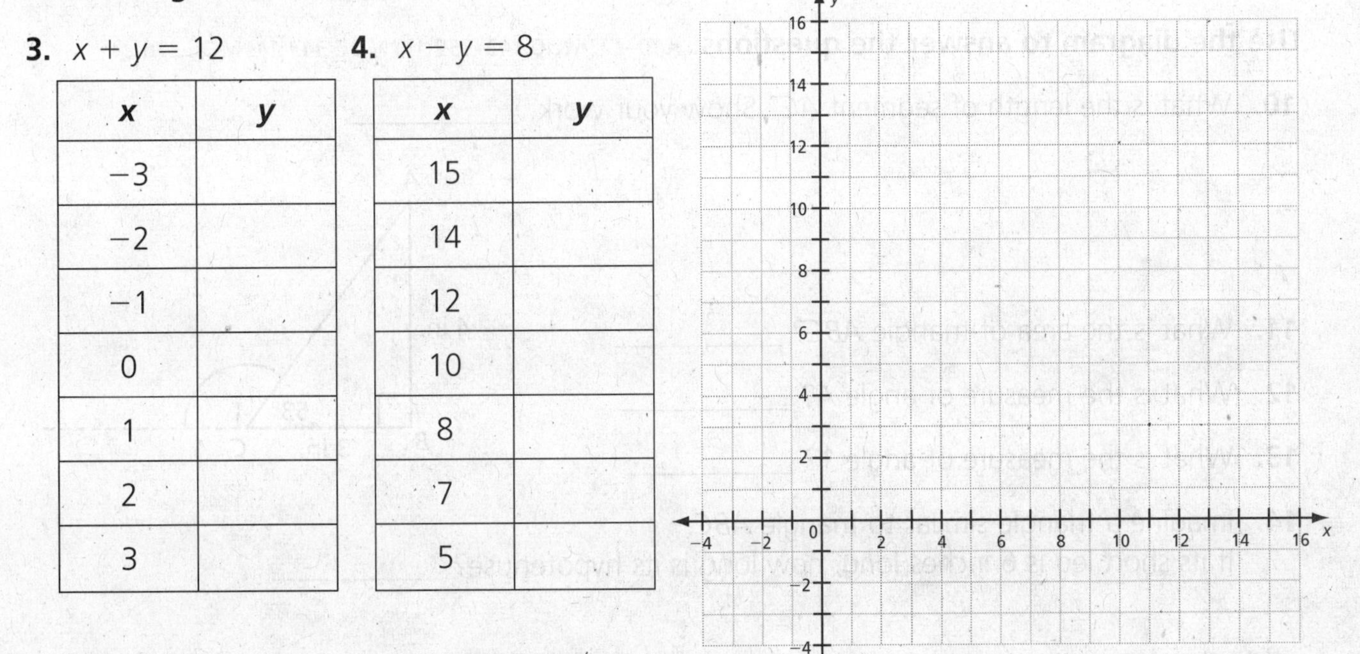

3. $x + y = 12$

x	y
−3	
−2	
−1	
0	
1	
2	
3	

4. $x - y = 8$

x	y
15	
14	
12	
10	
8	
7	
5	

Use the graphs for problems 3 and 4 to answer these questions. ◂5–6. MOC 248, 250

5. What word describes the type of functions you graphed? ____________________

6. Find the slope and describe its direction for each of the graphs.

$x + y = 12$: ____________________

$x - y = 8$: ____________________

GEOMETRY AND MEASUREMENT

Use the diagram to help you answer the questions. ◂7–9. MOC 394–396

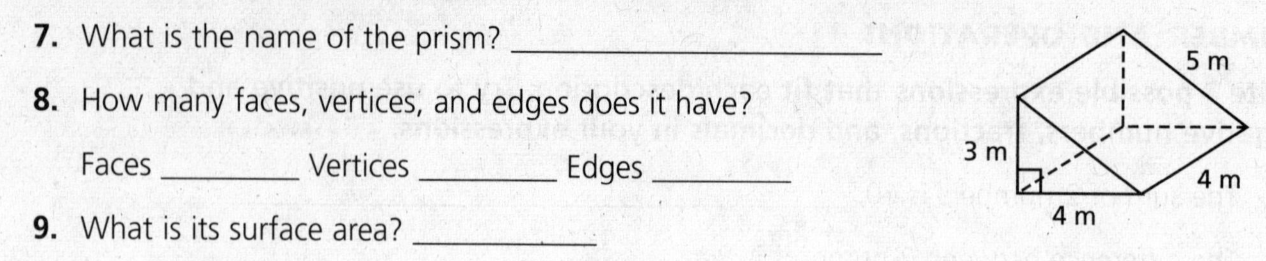

7. What is the name of the prism? ____________

8. How many faces, vertices, and edges does it have?

Faces ________ Vertices ________ Edges ________

9. What is its surface area? ____________

REVIEW

Use the diagram to answer the questions. ◂10–12. MOC 348–359 13. MOC 343 14. MOC 376

10. What is the length of segment *AC*? Show your work. ____________

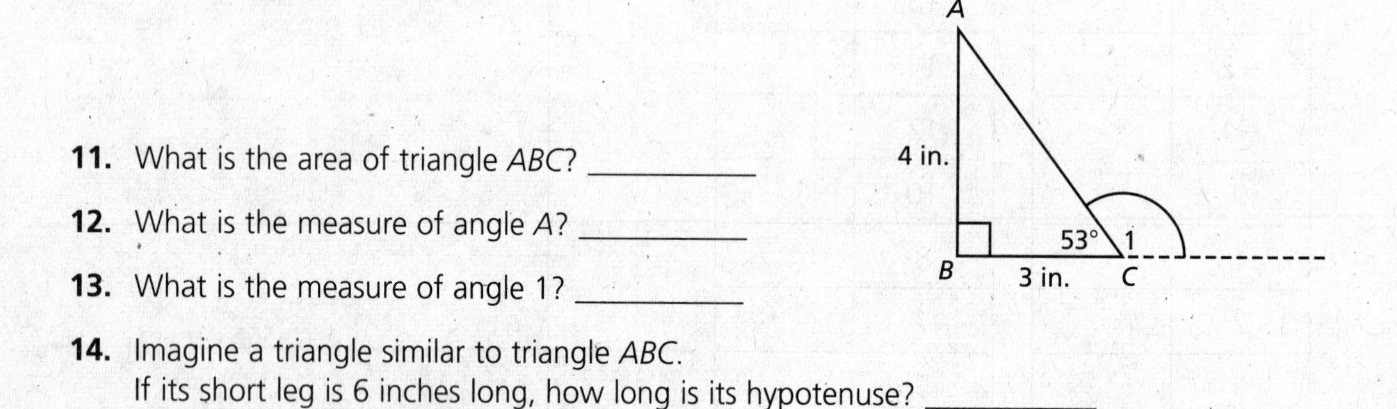

11. What is the area of triangle *ABC*? ____________

12. What is the measure of angle *A*? ____________

13. What is the measure of angle 1? ____________

14. Imagine a triangle similar to triangle *ABC*.
If its short leg is 6 inches long, how long is its hypotenuse? ____________

GLOSSARY TO GO

Review the definitions and illustrations you added to your Glossary this week.
Make additions or corrections if you need to.

Name ____

Problem Solving: More Bags of Apples

POSSIBLE STRATEGIES

- Guess, Check, and Revise
- Make a Model or Diagram
- Write an Equation
- Other: ____________

DIRECTIONS

- Solve the problem. Circle the strategies you used.
- Show your work and complete the answer.
- Assume the pans are balanced, each bag contains the same number of apples, and the number of apples is the same on both sides of the scale.

PROBLEM 1

On a balance scale, one side has 2 apples and 5 bags. The other side has 14 apples and 3 bags. How many apples are in each bag?

There are ________ apples in each bag.

PROBLEM 2

On a balance scale, one side has 2 bags and 9 apples. The other side has 16 apples and 1 bag. How many apples are in each bag?

There are ________ apples in each bag.

ANALYZE YOUR WORK

If you did not use the *Write an Equation* strategy, try to write one now for Problem 2.

____

Summer Success: Math

This week of summer school, one area of emphasis was expressions and equations. These basic building blocks of algebra are very important in school, but they're also useful any time you need to describe a relationship between numbers that can change. So, variable-rate mortgages, gasoline consumption, daily earnings for hourly pay, even your monthly cell phone bills, all can be described with expressions and equations.

If your child does chores or baby-sits to earn money, encourage good record-keeping and help him or her to set goals.

On the back of this page are some problems similar to ones your child did in class. Ask your child to show you how to solve them.

Enjoy your time with your child, and thank you for helping to strengthen your child's comfort with important math concepts.

Keeping Track of Earnings

1. Keep a graph of your hours and earnings on the refrigerator. That way, you might be able to figure out how much money you should expect to earn in several months.

2. If you charge $6.50 per hour, how much do you earn baby-sitting for 3 hours? What about 4 hours? What if you charge $7.00 per hour?

3. If your customers don't want to pay $7.00 per hour, what if you keep your $6.50 rate and insist on a 4-hour minimum job?

4. If you want to buy that $50 pair of pants, how many hours do you need to work to earn enough?

Show your child that you're proud of his or her progress. Remember that using math in the real world will help your child understand that studying math is important in school.

PRACTICE TODAY'S NUMBER $x > 5$

Name ______________________________

NUMBER AND OPERATIONS

Write 3 numbers that fit each inequality. ◀1–3. MOC 007, 258

1. $x > 6$ ______________________________
2. $x < 12$ ______________________________
3. $x \geq 7$ ______________________________

Graph each inequality on a number line. ◀4–5. MOC 258

4. $x > 6$

5. $x \leq 7$

PATTERNS AND ALGEBRA

Write an inequality for each statement. ◀6–10. MOC 007, 258

6. x is any number greater than 3 ________________
7. x is 5 or greater ________________
8. x is any number less than 2 ________________
9. x is 2 or less ________________
10. x is less than 3 and greater than -1 ________________

GEOMETRY AND MEASUREMENT

Draw the shape then answer the related question. ◀11–12. MOC 370, 374

11. Sketch a circle. Sketch 2 perpendicular diameters. Now sketch 2 more diameters so you have 8 approximately equal segments.

12. What would be the measure of each central angle if your drawing were precise?

____

REVIEW

Complete each table of values. Then answer the questions. ◂13–18. MOC 243, 245–247

13. $y = -4x$

x	y
−2	
−1	
0	
1	
2	

14. $y = 1.5x$

x	y
−4	
−2	
0	
2	
4	

15. What do you expect the graph of the equation in problem 13 to look like? Be sure to mention slope.

____

16. What do you expect the graph of the equation in problem 14 to look like? Be sure to mention slope.

____

17. Where will the 2 lines intersect? __________

18. Graph and label the functions in problems 13 and 14 on the coordinate grid.

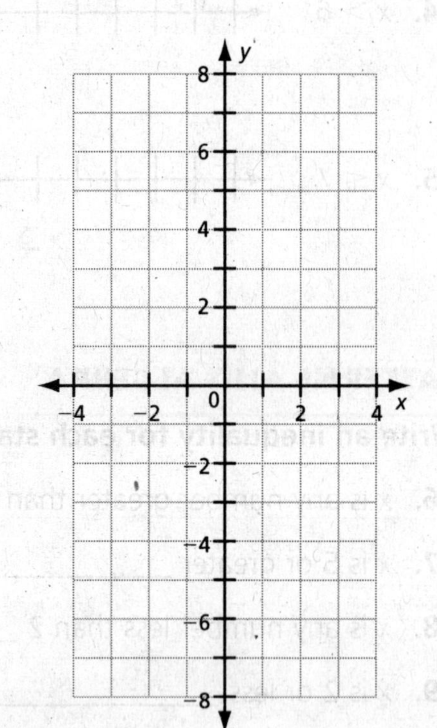

GLOSSARY TO GO

Write definitions and draw pictures illustrating new math terms. The vocabulary should be covered in your class time, so you should be familiar with most of the terms.

GAME

Which Fraction?

Object: Make and add fractions in order to get a final sum near 8.

MATERIALS

Two 1–6 number cubes, pencils

DIRECTIONS

1. If you are Player 2, turn to page 130. You will share the Recording Sheets on this page.
2. Decide whether to make a fraction greater than 1 or less than 1 when you roll the number cubes. Record that on your Recording Sheet. **Tell why** you made that decision. **(This is my first turn, and even if I get 6 and 1, I won't be too close to 8, so I'll use *greater than*.)**
3. Roll the number cubes and make a fraction. If your value is exactly 1, you lose your turn.
4. Take turns choosing *greater than* or *less than*, rolling the cubes, and making fractions. Add your fraction for each round to the amount in the *Running Total* column.
5. After 4 rounds, if your running total is closer to but still less than 8, you win.

Round	> or < ?	Fractions	Running Total
1	> 1	$\frac{4}{2} = 2$	2
2	> 1	$\frac{6}{5} = 1\frac{1}{5}$	$3\frac{1}{5}$
3	> 1	$\frac{6}{2} = 3$	$6\frac{1}{5}$
4			

Which Fraction? Recording Sheet

Player 1 ____________________

Round	> or < ?	Fractions	Running Total
1			
2			
3			
4			

Round	> or < ?	Fractions	Running Total
1			
2			
3			
4			

Round	> or < ?	Fractions	Running Total
1			
2			
3			
4			

Round	> or < ?	Fractions	Running Total
1			
2			
3			
4			

Player 2 ____________________

Round	> or < ?	Fractions	Running Total
1			
2			
3			
4			

Round	> or < ?	Fractions	Running Total
1			
2			
3			
4			

Round	> or < ?	Fractions	Running Total
1			
2			
3			
4			

Round	> or < ?	Fractions	Running Total
1			
2			
3			
4			

Name ______________________________

Finding Probability

What is the probability of choosing a red or blue counter after 10 picks from a bag of 20 red, blue, green, and yellow counters?

DIRECTIONS

- Work with a partner.
- Mix 5 each of red, blue, green, and yellow counters in a bag.
- Complete the first row of the chart on page 132.
- Pick one counter at a time from the bag and fill in the chart after each turn. Do not replace the counters in the bag. Record the data for 10 turns.
- Answer the questions to analyze the data.

ANALYZE THE DATA

1. Before picking any counters from the bag, what is the probability of choosing each color?

____

____

2. After the first turn, what is the probability of picking a red counter?

____

____

3. After the first turn, what is the probability of picking a blue counter?

____

4. After the first turn, what is the probability of picking red or blue?

____

____

5. After the tenth turn, what is the probability of picking a red or a blue counter?

____

____

Finding Probability

Turn	Number of Red Counters in Bag	Number of Blue Counters in Bag	Total Number of Counters in Bag	Probability of Picking Red or Blue on Next Turn
Start	5	5	20	$\frac{10}{20} = \frac{1}{2}$
1			19	
2			18	
3			17	
4			16	
5			15	
6			14	
7			13	
8			12	
9			11	
10			10	

Name ______________________________

NUMBER AND OPERATIONS

Complete the table of values. Answer the related question. ◀1–2. MOC 243, 246, 548

1. $y = 3^x$

x	y
3	
2	
1	
0	
−1	
−2	
−3	

2. Will the graph of $y = 3^x$ be a straight line? How do you know?

____

____

PATTERNS AND ALGEBRA

Continue the patterns. ◀3–5. MOC 073, 548

3. 1, 3, 9, 27, ________, ________

4. 1, 4, 16, 64, ________, ________

5. The first term of a pattern described by the expression 3^{-n} is $3^{-1} = \frac{1}{3^1} = \frac{1}{3}$.
Write the next 3 terms.

________, ________, ________

GEOMETRY AND MEASUREMENT

Use the diagrams. Show your work. Use 3.14 for π. ◂6–8. MOC 403, 407–408, 418

6. The volume of the cone is about ________________.

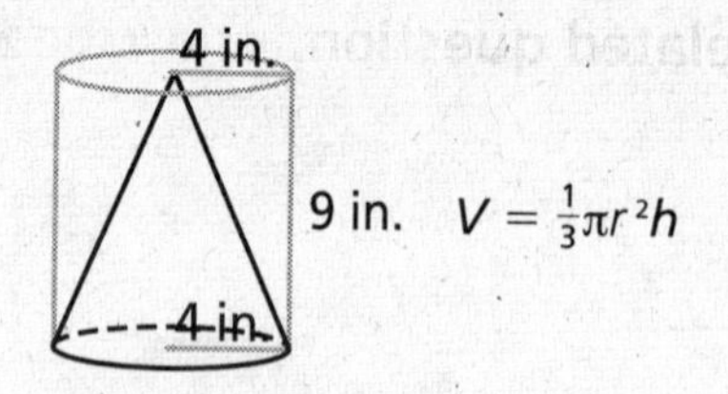

$V = \frac{1}{3}\pi r^2 h$

7. The volume of the pyramid is ________________.

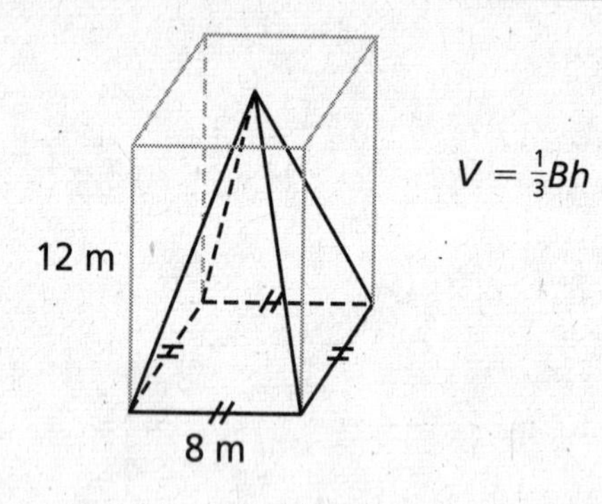

$V = \frac{1}{3}Bh$

8. Find the number of faces, vertices, and edges on the pyramid.

Faces: __________ Vertices: __________ Edges: __________

REVIEW

Use >, <, or = to compare the fractions. ◂9–12. MOC 039–040

9. $\frac{1}{2}$ ______ $\frac{1}{3}$

10. $\frac{1}{2}$ ______ $\frac{2}{3}$

11. $\frac{1}{2}$ ______ $\frac{3}{6}$

12. $\frac{2}{9}$ ______ $\frac{5}{9}$

Evaluate each expression. ◂13–18. MOC 106–107, 134–135, 160–162, 187–188, 191

13. $\frac{2}{7} + \frac{3}{7}$ ____________

14. $\frac{1}{3} + \frac{3}{4}$ ____________

15. $\frac{1}{6} - \frac{5}{6}$ ____________

16. $\frac{1}{5} \times \frac{3}{5}$ ____________

17. $\frac{3}{4} \div \frac{3}{8}$ ____________

18. $\frac{2}{9} \div \frac{2}{27}$ ____________

GLOSSARY TO GO

Write definitions and draw pictures illustrating new math terms. The vocabulary should be covered in your class time, so you should be familiar with most of the terms.

Name ______________________________

More Probability

How does the probability of picking 2 red counters from the same bag compare to the probability of picking a red counter from each of 2 different bags?

DIRECTIONS

- Work with a partner. Record your results on page 136.
- Mix 5 red and 5 blue counters in Bag 1.
- Mix 5 red and 5 yellow counters in Bag 2.

PART A

- On each turn, pick one counter from Bag 1. Keep that counter and pick another from Bag 1. Fill in the chart for that turn.
- Return both counters to Bag 1. Record data for 9 turns.

PART B

- On each turn, pick one counter from each bag, then fill in the chart for that turn.
- Return the counters to the correct bag. Record data for 12 turns.

ANALYZE THE DATA

1. What is the theoretical probability of picking a red counter and then picking a second red counter from Bag 1? Are those events dependent or independent?

   ____

2. What is the theoretical probability of picking a red counter from Bag 1 and a red counter from Bag 2? Are those events dependent or independent?

   ____

3. Compare the results of your trials to theoretical probability.

   ____

   ____

   ____

More Probability

PART A CHART

Pick 2 Counters from Bag 1

Theoretical probability of picking red, then red:

______

Turn	Red, Then Red
1	
2	
3	
4	
5	
6	
7	
8	
9	

Experimental results: ______

PART B CHART

Pick 1 Counter from Each Bag

Theoretical probability of picking red, then red:

______

Turn	Red, Then Red
1	
2	
3	
4	
5	
6	
7	
8	
9	
10	
11	
12	

Experimental results: ______

PRACTICE TODAY'S NUMBER $\frac{a}{b}$

Name ______________________________

NUMBER AND OPERATIONS

Answer each question for *a* > *b*, when neither *a* nor *b* is 0. ◂1–4. MOC 028

1. What does $a > b$ mean?

____

2. Which is greater $\frac{1}{a}$ or $\frac{1}{b}$? How do you know?

____

____

3. Is $\frac{a}{b}$ greater than or less than 1? How do you know?

____

____

4. Is $\frac{a}{b}$ greater than or less than $\frac{b}{a}$? How do you know?

____

Simplify each expression. ◂5–10. MOC 028, 107, 162

5. $\frac{a}{b} + \frac{a}{b}$ __________ **6.** $\frac{1}{a} + \frac{1}{b}$ __________ **7.** $\frac{1}{a} - \frac{5}{a}$ __________

8. $\frac{3}{a} - \frac{4}{b}$ __________ **9.** $\frac{1}{a} \times \frac{3}{a}$ __________ **10.** $\frac{2}{a} \times \frac{5}{b}$ __________

PATTERNS AND ALGEBRA

Use the diagram to answer the questions. ◂11–13. MOC 248

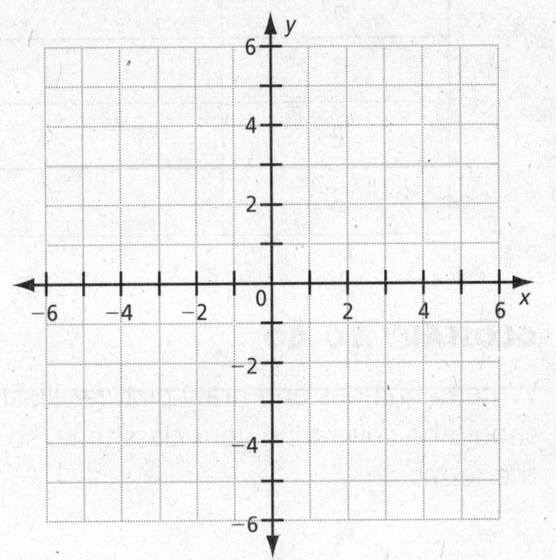

11. Which graph has a negative slope?

____

12. Both graphs cross the *y*-axis at the same point. What is this point and what is the special name for its *y*-value?

____

13. Write an equation for line B. ______________________________

GEOMETRY AND MEASUREMENT

Use this diagram of similar triangles to answer the questions. ◀14–17. MOC 376

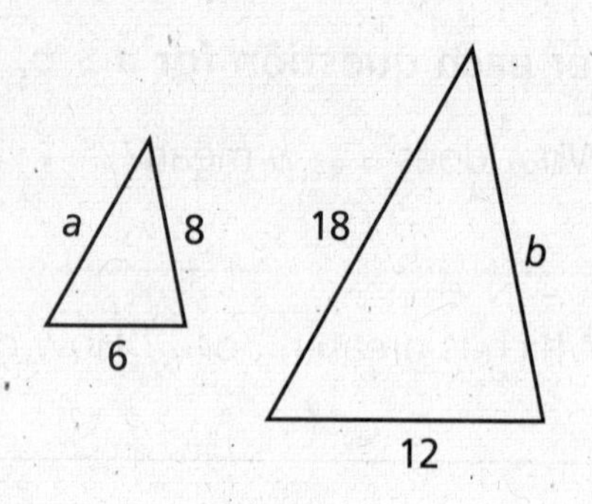

14. What is the relationship between the corresponding sides of similar polygons?

____

15. What is the ratio of the corresponding sides for which you know the length?

____

16. What is the measure of side *a*? ________

17. What is the measure of side *b*? ________

REVIEW

Write the value of each expression. ◀18–21. MOC 207–209

18. 1^{10} ________

19. 10^3 ________

20. $2 + 2^3$ ________

21. $3 + 2^3 \times 5$ ________

Complete the table. ◀22. MOC 073, 206–209, 548

22.

x	$x - 3$	x^4	4^x
−3			
−2			
−1			
1			
2			
3			

GLOSSARY TO GO

Write definitions and draw pictures illustrating new math terms. The vocabulary should be covered in your class time, so you should be familiar with most of the terms.

Equate That Mosquito

Object: Plot lines that intersect points on your partner's targets.

If I just use one of my numbers, I can make a horizontal line, y = −2, that will hit your mosquito.

MATERIALS

Two number cubes numbered 1, −1, 2, −2, 3, −3;
pencils in 2 colors; paper

DIRECTIONS

1. If you are Player 2, turn to page 139A. You will share the recording sheet on this page. Share a grid on the Game Board on page 139B. If you are Player 1, you play to the left of the *y*-axis. If you are Player 2, you play to the right of the *y*-axis. Choose your pencil color and shade any two 1×1 squares on your side of the grid. These are your mosquitoes.
2. Roll the number cubes. Decide how to use any or all of the numbers in a linear equation. The numbers can multiply *x* or be added to or subtracted from *x*. One of them can even be the value of *x*, or, you might use both of them to form a fraction. **Tell why** you made your decision. **(If my equation is $y = x + 3$, it will intersect your mosquito.)**
3. Plot your points and draw your line. Extend it to the edges of the grid.
4. Take turns. If you are first to intersect both of your partner's mosquitoes twice, you win.

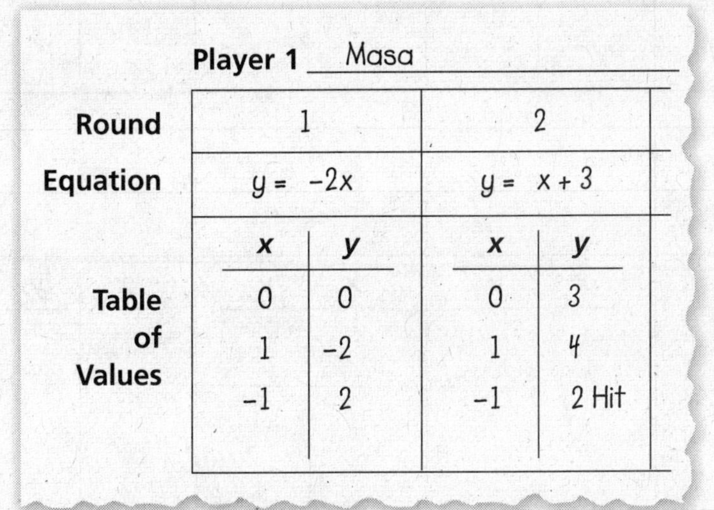

Player 1 Masa

Round	1		2	
Equation	y = −2x		y = x + 3	
Table of Values	**x**	**y**	**x**	**y**
	0	0	0	3
	1	−2	1	4
	−1	2	−1	2 Hit

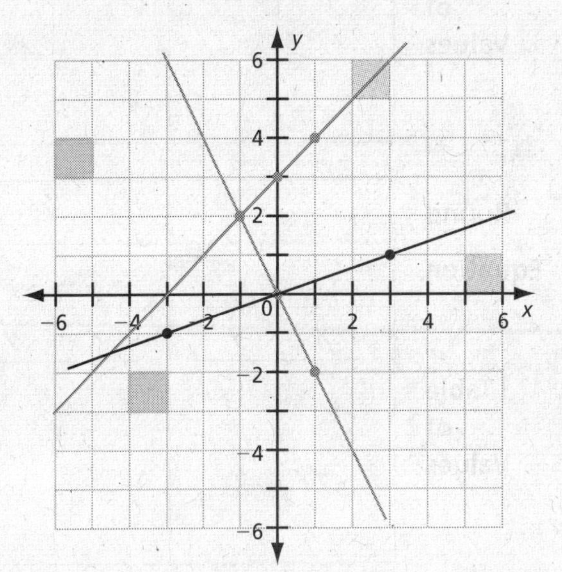

Coordinate Grids Recording Sheet

Player 1 ______________________________

Round					
Equation					
Table of Values	x | y	x | y	x | y	x | y	x | y

Round					
Equation					
Table of Values	x | y	x | y	x | y	x | y	x | y

Player 2 ______________________________

Round					
Equation					
Table of Values	x | y	x | y	x | y	x | y	x | y

Round					
Equation					
Table of Values	x | y	x | y	x | y	x | y	x | y

Coordinate Grids Game Board

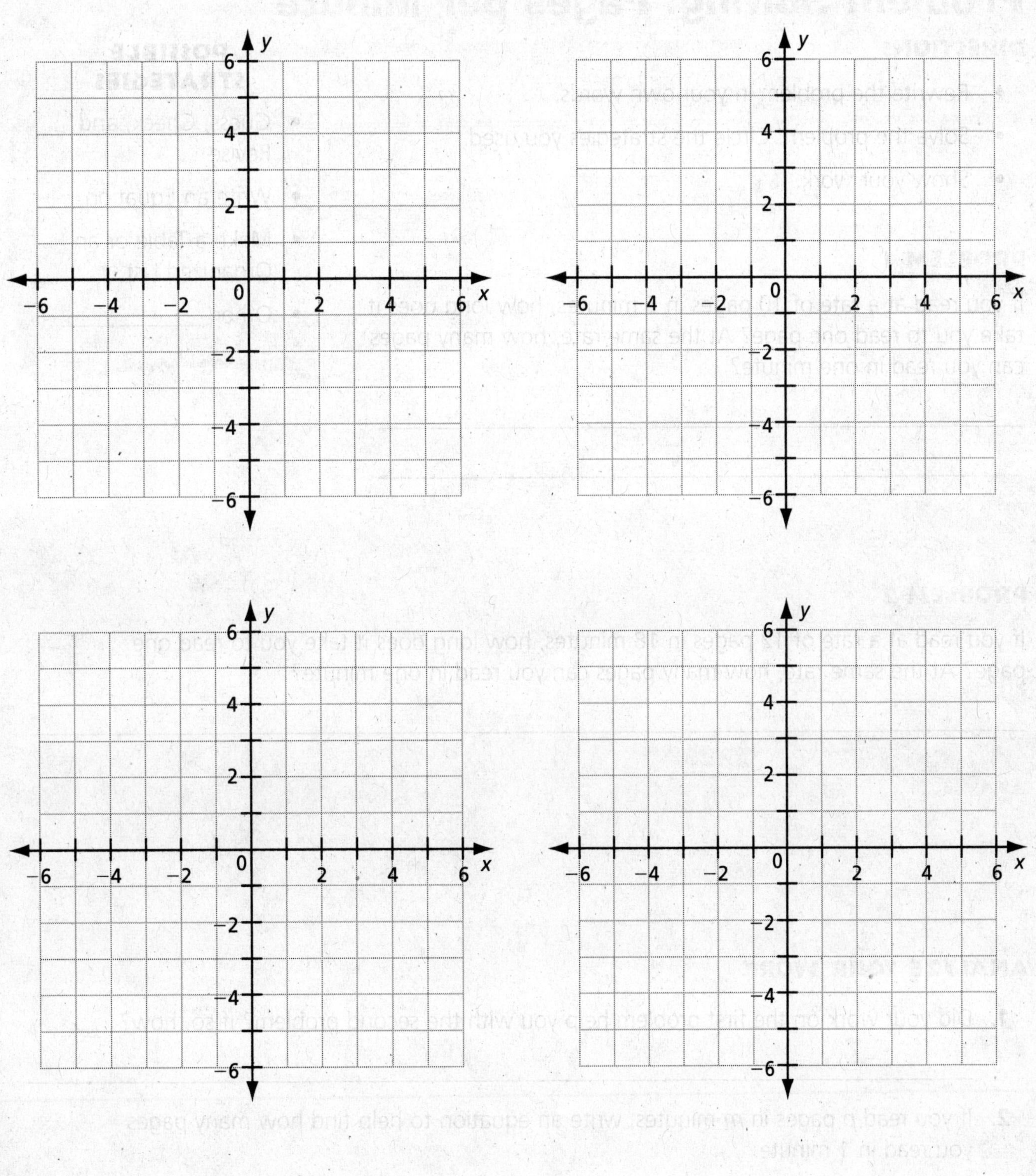

Name ____________________

Problem Solving: Pages per Minute

DIRECTIONS

- Rewrite the problem in your own words.
- Solve the problem. Circle the strategies you used.
- Show your work.

POSSIBLE STRATEGIES

- Guess, Check, and Revise
- Write an Equation
- Make a Table or an Organized List
- Other ____________

PROBLEM 1

If you read at a rate of 10 pages in 5 minutes, how long does it take you to read one page? At the same rate, how many pages can you read in one minute?

____

____

PROBLEM 2

If you read at a rate of 12 pages in 18 minutes, how long does it take you to read one page? At the same rate, how many pages can you read in one minute?

____

ANALYZE YOUR WORK

1. Did your work on the first problem help you with the second problem? If so, how?

   ____

2. If you read p pages in m minutes, write an equation to help find how many pages you read in 1 minute.

   ____

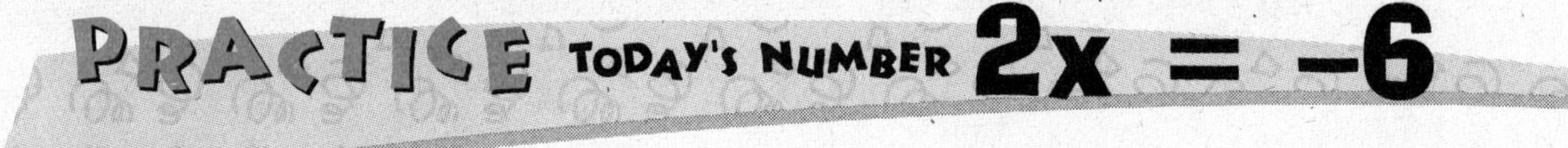

Name ______________________________

NUMBER AND OPERATIONS

Write each number by the correct dot on the number line. There are more dots than numbers, so be careful. ◂1–4. MOC 049

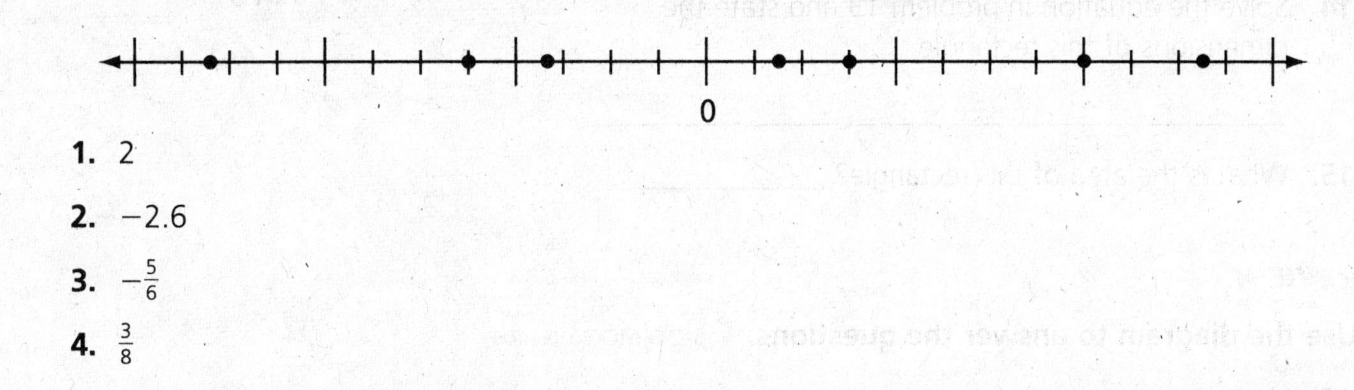

1. 2
2. −2.6
3. $-\frac{5}{6}$
4. $\frac{3}{8}$

PATTERNS AND ALGEBRA

Find the value of x. Show your work. ◂5–10. MOC 239–242

5. $3x - 4 = 8$; $x =$ ______
6. $2x + 3 = 4x$; $x =$ ______
7. $5x + 2 = 3x$; $x =$ ______
8. $x^2 + 2 = 6$; $x =$ ______
9. $5x + 6 = 16$; $x =$ ______
10. $4x + 2x = 42$; $x =$ ______

Write an equation, and then solve the problem. ◂11–12. MOC 205–209, 239–242

11. Danielle is 13 years more than twice as old as James. Danielle is 43 years old. How old is James?

____

12. Nine more than a number equals 4 times that number. What is the number?

____

MEASUREMENT

Use the diagram to solve the problems. ◂13–15. MOC 205–209, 239–242, 365

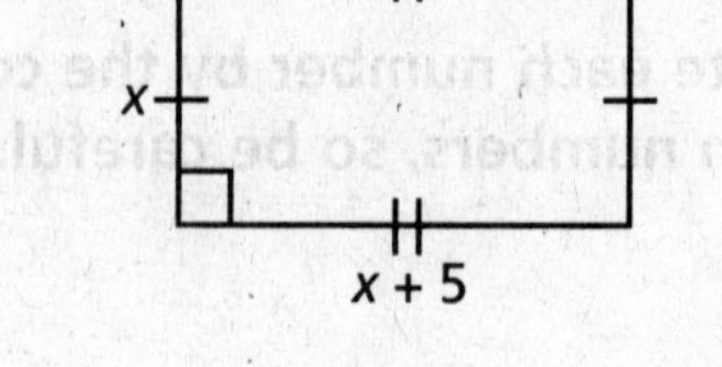

13. The perimeter of this rectangle is 34 centimeters. Write an equation that could be used to find its dimensions.

____

14. Solve the equation in problem 13 and state the dimensions of this rectangle.

____

15. What is the area of this rectangle? ____________

REVIEW

Use the diagram to answer the questions. ◂16–24. MOC 399–401

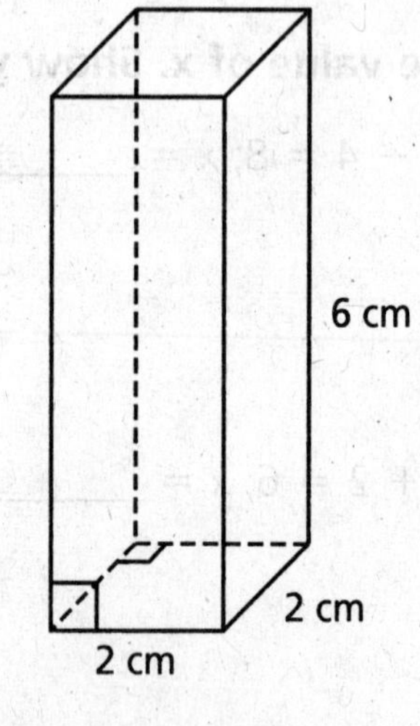

16. How many vertices? __________

17. How many edges? __________

18. How many lateral faces? __________

19. How many bases? __________

20. Name a polygon that describes the lateral faces.

____

21. What is the area of each of the faces? __________

22. Name a polygon that describes the bases.

____

23. What is the area of each of the bases? ____________

24. What is the surface area of this figure? ____________

GLOSSARY TO GO

Write definitions and draw pictures illustrating new math terms. The vocabulary should be covered in your class time, so you should be familiar with most of the terms.

Name ____________________

Problem Solving: Yellow and Green Stamps

DIRECTIONS

- Rewrite the problem in your own words.
- Solve the problem. Circle the strategies you used.
- Show your work.

POSSIBLE STRATEGIES

- Guess, Check, and Revise
- Write an Equation
- Make a Model or a Diagram
- Make a Graph
- Other ____________

PROBLEM 1

One yellow stamp is worth one green stamp plus \$1. Two green stamps are worth one yellow stamp plus \$2. What is the value of each stamp?

PROBLEM 2

Three yellow stamps are worth 4 green stamps plus \$4. Two green stamps are worth one yellow stamp plus \$2. What is the value of each stamp?

ANALYZE YOUR WORK

1. Did your work on the first problem help you with the second problem? If so, how?

____

2. If you didn't use the *Write an Equation* strategy for Problem 2, write equations for the problem now.

____

Name ______________________________

NUMBER AND OPERATIONS

Write 3 possible expressions that fit each description. Include integers and rational numbers. ◀1–2. MOC 132–136

1. The difference between 2 numbers is 6. ______________________________

2. The difference between 2 numbers is 1. ______________________________

Complete each table of values. Then answer the related questions. ◀3–4. MOC 243, 5–7. MOC 248, 250

3. $y = x - 10$

x	y
−6	
−2	
0	
2	
6	

4. $y = x + 10$

x	y
−10	
−6	
−2	
0	
2	

5. Will the slope of the graph of each equation be positive or negative?

   $y = x - 10$ __________ $y = x + 10$ __________

6. How can you tell, without graphing, whether the point (3, 0) lies on either graph?

   ____

   ____

7. What word describes the type of functions in problems 4 and 5? __________

PATTERNS AND ALGEBRA

Solve the related problems. ◀8–9. MOC 238–240

8. Write an equation that represents the difference between twice a number and 8 more than the number.

   ____

9. For the equation in problem 8; what is the value of y when x is 2.5? __________

GEOMETRY

Name and give some attributes of each shape. ◂10. MOC 363 11. MOC 394

10.

11.

_______________ _______________

_______________ _______________

_______________ _______________

_______________ _______________

REVIEW

Solve these problems. ◂12–17. MOC 428–434

12. It takes you 4 hours to hike 6 miles. At that rate, how many hours does it take you to hike one mile? _______________

13. At that rate, how far can you hike in one hour? _______________

14. Karen stood on the corner and counted passing cars for 3 hours. Her hourly counts were 70, 80, and 90 cars. How many will she need to see during the fourth hour for her mean to be 85 cars per hour?

____

15. Karen actually counted 88 cars during the fourth hour. What is the mean number of cars per hour?

____

16. What is the median number of cars per hour? _______________

17. What is the range of cars per hour? _______________

GLOSSARY TO GO

Review the definitions and illustrations you added to your Glossary this week. Make additions or corrections if you need to.

Name ______________________________

Problem Solving: T-Shirts and Tank Tops

DIRECTIONS

- Rewrite the problem in your own words.
- Solve the problem. Circle the strategies you used.
- Show your work.

POSSIBLE STRATEGIES

- Guess, Check, and Revise
- Write an Equation
- Make a Table or an Organized List
- Make a Graph
- Other ___________

PROBLEM 1

A tank top costs \$6 less than a T-shirt. Four tank tops cost \$10 more than 2 T-shirts. How much does each type of top cost?

PROBLEM 2

A tank top costs \$6 less than a T-shirt. One T-shirt costs \$7 less than 3 tank tops. How much does each type of top cost?

ANALYZE YOUR WORK

1. Did your work on the first problem help you with the second problem? If so, how?

____

2. If you didn't use the *Write an Equation* strategy for Problem 2, write an equation for the problem now.

____

NEWSLETTER

Summer Success: Math

This week, your child has been working with all kinds of numbers in inequalities, expressions, and equations. We've also seen that some equations can be graphed as a line and some will make a curve. Your child has learned to tell, just by looking at the equation, a number of things about what its graph will look like.

You can help your child get comfortable with the relationships between numbers by reading and discussing newspaper and magazine articles that use numbers and graphs to make a point.

On the back of this page is a math trick your child can try on you and your family. It reinforces ideas about how number relationships work.

Enjoy your time with your child, and thank you for helping to strengthen your child's comfort with important math concepts.

Number Trick

MATERIALS

paper, pencil

GET READY

Before you perform this trick, practice using mental math to quickly find sums of 999. If one addend is 348, write what you need to add to each digit to get 9. That's 651. If one addend is 940, the other is 59. Practice with these first addends:

420 + ________ = 999   502 + ________ = 999

391 + ________ = 999   789 + ________ = 999

Now you're ready.

DIRECTIONS

1. Ask a friend or family member to write two 3-digit numbers. Tell them you'll add 2 numbers to the list and then they'll write one more 3-digit number.
2. Study the first 2 numbers. Write numbers that you can add to those 2 numbers to make a sum of 999.
   For example, if the numbers are
   458
   689
   then you write
   541
   310
   You know that the sum of these 4 numbers is 999 × 2, which is 2 less than 2,000, but they might not catch on to what you've done.
3. Now ask the friend or family member to write another 3-digit number and find the sum of all 5 numbers. Offer them the pencil and paper. You won't need it.
4. Remember, you know that the sum of the first 4 numbers is 2 less than 2,000. It should be easy for you use mental math to add the fifth number to 2,000, subtract 2, and impress everyone in the room!

Show your child that you're proud of his or her accomplishments. The math in this year's summer school was challenging but very useful.

GLOSSARY TO GO

A

absolute value

angle

arc

A

B

base

C

coordinate grid

cylinder

C

C

D

E

exponent

exponential function

E

F

G

H

I

inequality

integer

I

J K L

length

M N

O

origin

P

percent

prism

proportion

P

Pythagorean Theorem

P

Q R

rational number

repeating decimal

right triangle

Q R

S

similar

symmetry

S

T

transversal

T

U V W X Y Z

vertical angles

POST TEST

Name ______________________________

NUMBER

Choose the best answer or write a response for each question.

1. Which diagram shows 0.2 of the stars shaded?

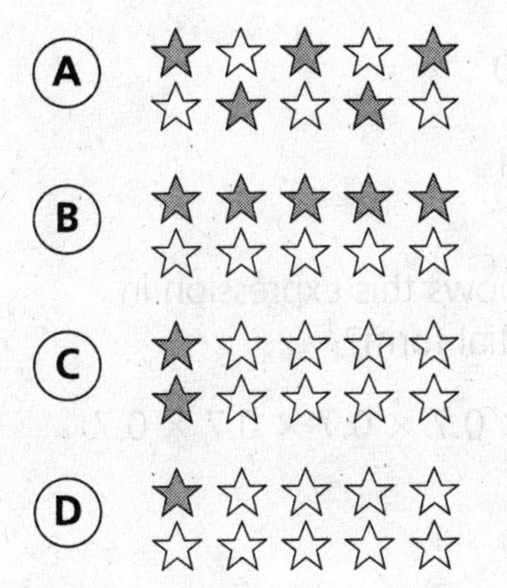

Ⓐ
Ⓑ
Ⓒ
Ⓓ

2. What is 0.5 written as a fraction?

Ⓐ $\frac{5}{2}$

Ⓑ $\frac{1}{2}$

Ⓒ $\frac{2}{5}$

Ⓓ $\frac{1}{4}$

3. What is $3\frac{1}{3}$ written as a percent?

Ⓐ $0.\overline{3}\%$

Ⓑ $\overline{3}.0\%$

Ⓒ $3.\overline{3}\%$

Ⓓ $33.\overline{3}\%$

4. What is the opposite of the integer −5?

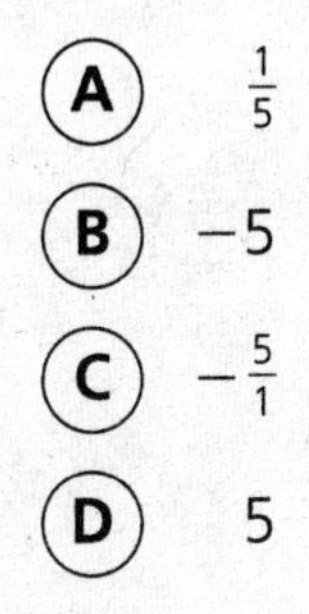

Ⓐ $\frac{1}{5}$

Ⓑ −5

Ⓒ $-\frac{5}{1}$

Ⓓ 5

5. Which group of numbers is listed from greatest to least?

Ⓐ $-\frac{1}{8}, -\frac{1}{4}, \frac{1}{3}, \frac{1}{2}$

Ⓑ $\frac{1}{2}, \frac{1}{3}, -\frac{1}{8}, -\frac{1}{4}$

Ⓒ $-\frac{1}{4}, -\frac{1}{8}, \frac{1}{3}, \frac{1}{2}$

Ⓓ $\frac{1}{2}, -\frac{1}{4}, -\frac{1}{8}, -\frac{1}{3}$

6. Which expression does **not** have the same value as the others?

Ⓐ 12×1

Ⓑ $|-12|$

Ⓒ $-3 \times (-4)$

Ⓓ 12×-1

Name ______________________________

OPERATIONS

7. What is the difference?

$-86 - 41 = $ ____

Ⓐ -127

Ⓑ -45

Ⓒ 45

Ⓓ 127

8. What is $\sqrt{64}$?

Ⓐ 64 and -64

Ⓑ 8 and -8

Ⓒ -8 only

Ⓓ 8 only

9. What is the missing factor?

$-3 \times$ ____ $= -75$

Ⓐ 25

Ⓑ -25

Ⓒ -50

Ⓓ Not Given

10. What is the quotient?

$-\frac{1}{3} \div (-\frac{1}{3})$

Ⓐ 3

Ⓑ 1

Ⓒ 0

Ⓓ -1

11. Which shows this expression in exponential form?

$0.7 \times 0.7 \times 0.7 \times 0.7 \times 0.7$

Ⓐ 0.7^{-5}

Ⓑ 0.7^{5}

Ⓒ 7.0^{5}

Ⓓ 7.0^{3}

12. Which shows this number in scientific notation?

6,510,000

Ⓐ 651×10^{4}

Ⓑ 65.1×10^{5}

Ⓒ 6.51×10^{6}

Ⓓ 0.651×10^{7}

Name ___________________________

PATTERNS AND ALGEBRA

13. Continue the pattern.

23, 15, 7, −1, −9, ___

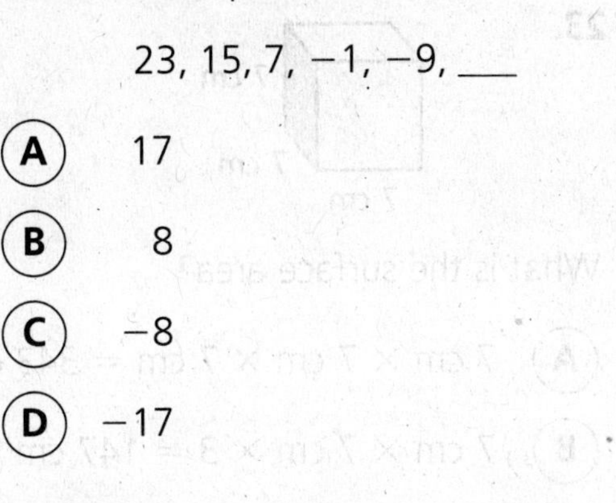

(A) 17

(B) 8

(C) −8

(D) −17

14. What rule is followed to create the pattern?

−10, −4, 2, 8

(A) Add 6.

(B) Add 4.

(C) Add −4.

(D) Add −6.

15. Write an equation to find the measure of the third angle.

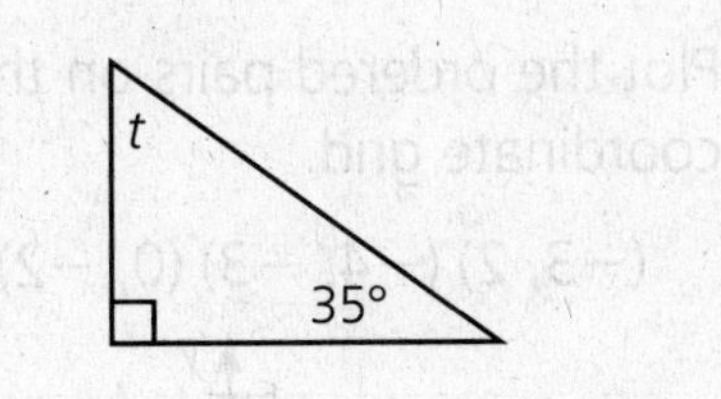

Answer: ___________________________

16. Solve for *n*.

$\frac{1}{5}n = -20$

(A) $n = 100$

(B) $n = 4$

(C) $n = -100$

(D) $n = -120$

17. Use the grid to graph the equation.

$y = -2x + 1$

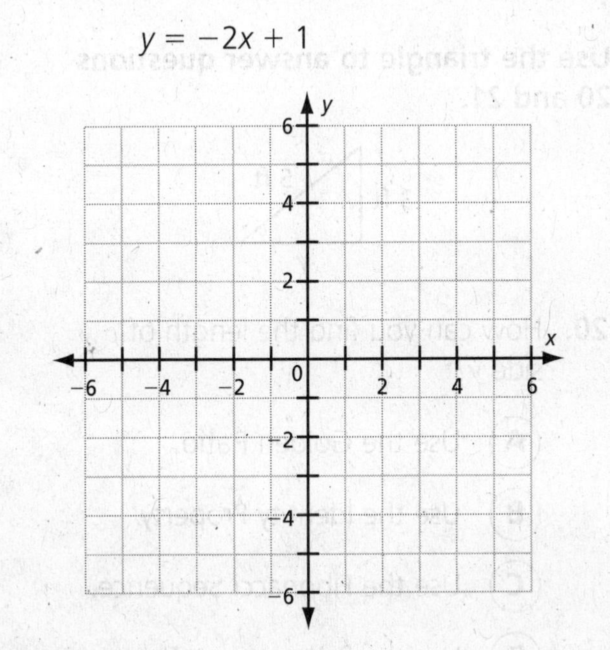

18. What is the *y*-intercept?

(A) the point where a line crosses the *y*-axis

(B) the *y*-coordinate of the point where a line crosses the *y*-axis

(C) the slope of a line

(D) the ordered pair (0, 0)

Name ______________________________

GEOMETRY AND MEASUREMENT

19. Which diagram shows a pair of complementary angles?

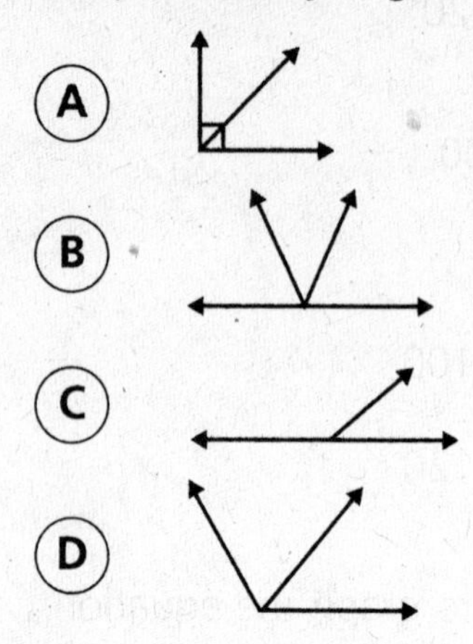

Use the triangle to answer questions 20 and 21.

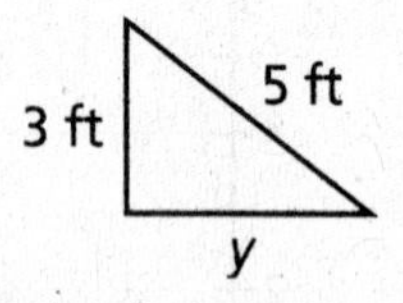

20. How can you find the length of side *y*?

(A) Use the Golden Ratio.

(B) Use the Identity Property.

(C) Use the Fibonacci Sequence.

(D) Use the Pythagorean Theorem.

21. Suppose $y = 4$ feet. What is the area of the triangle?

(A) $\frac{1}{2}(4 \text{ ft} \times 3 \text{ ft}) = 6 \text{ ft}^2$

(B) $3 \text{ ft} + 4 \text{ ft} + 5 \text{ ft} = 12 \text{ ft}$

(C) $\frac{1}{2}(4 \text{ ft} \times 5 \text{ ft}) = 10 \text{ ft}^2$

(D) $3 \text{ ft} \times 4 \text{ ft} \times 5 \text{ ft} = 60 \text{ ft}^3$

Use the cube to answer questions 22 and 23.

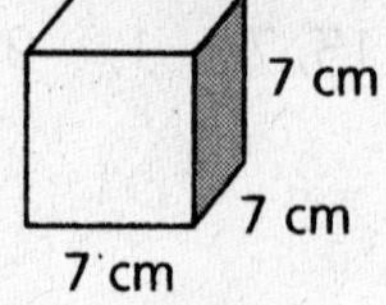

22. What is the surface area?

(A) $7 \text{ cm} \times 7 \text{ cm} \times 7 \text{ cm} = 343 \text{ cm}^3$

(B) $7 \text{ cm} \times 7 \text{ cm} \times 3 = 147 \text{ cm}^2$

(C) $7 \text{ cm} \times 7 \text{ cm} \times 6 = 294 \text{ cm}^2$

(D) $7 \text{ cm} + 7 \text{ cm} + 7 \text{ cm} = 21 \text{ cm}$

23. What is the volume?

(A) $7 \text{ cm} \times 7 \text{ cm} \times 7 \text{ cm} = 343 \text{ cm}^3$

(B) $7 \text{ cm} \times 7 \text{ cm} \times 6 = 294 \text{ cm}^2$

(C) $7 \text{ cm} + 7 \text{ cm} + 7 \text{ cm} + 7 \text{ cm} = 28 \text{ cm}$

(D) $7 \text{ cm} + 7 \text{ cm} \times 5 \text{ cm} = 7 \text{ cm} + 35 \text{ cm}^2$

24. Plot the ordered pairs on the coordinate grid.

$(-3, 2)\ (-4, -3)\ (0, -2)\ (4, 1)$

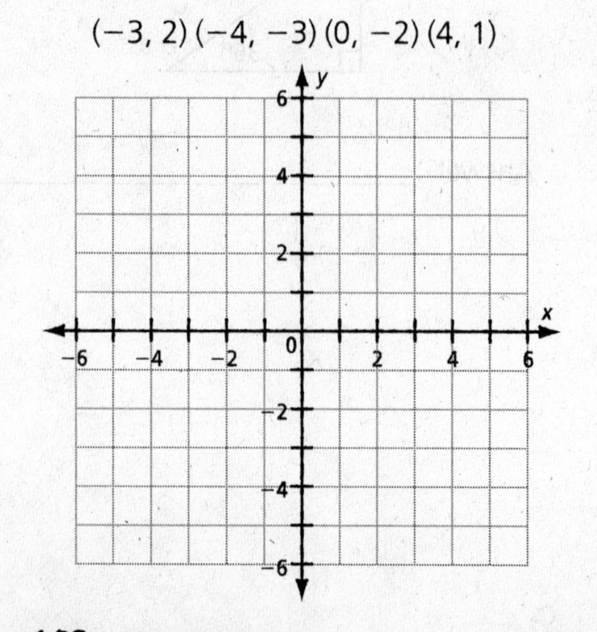

Name ______________________________

DATA

Use the stem-and-leaf plot to answer questions 25–28.

Running Times (sec)

Stems	Leaves
9	1 3 3
8	0 0 2 4
7	0 1 2 5

25. Make a key that shows that the stems are tens and the leaves are ones.

Answer: ______________________

26. What is the median of the running times?

Ⓐ 80 seconds

Ⓑ 81 seconds

Ⓒ 82 seconds

Ⓓ 84 seconds

27. What is the mean running time?

Ⓐ 93 seconds

Ⓑ 82 seconds

Ⓒ 81 seconds

Ⓓ 80 seconds

28. Make a line plot with the running times.

29. If there are 5 red counters, 5 blue ones, and 6 green ones in a bag, what is the probability that you'll pick a red counter?

Ⓐ $\frac{5}{11}$

Ⓑ $\frac{5}{16}$

Ⓒ $\frac{1}{5}$

Ⓓ $\frac{1}{16}$

30. Which kind of graph is best for showing change over time?

Ⓐ a stem-and-leaf plot

Ⓑ a circle graph

Ⓒ a line graph

Ⓓ a box-and-whisker plot

Name ______________________________

PROBLEM SOLVING

31. Each variable stands for one, and only one, integer. Find the values of *a*, *b*, and *c*.

$a + 6 = b$

$c - 2 = b$

$a + b = 14$

Show your work.

Answer: ______________________

32. Use the diagram to answer the questions.

A. Write an equation to describe the diagram. Show your work.

Answer: ______________________

B. What is the weight of 1 banana in terms of apples? Show your work.

Answer: ______________________

C. What is the weight of 1 apple in terms of bananas? Show your work.

Answer: ______________________